T0094585

Boleros

for the

Disenchanted

AND OTHER PLAYS

·)|(·

Boleros

for the

Disenchanted

AND OTHER PLAYS

·)⁞(·

José Rivera

THEATRE COMMUNICATIONS GROUP
NEW YORK
2012

Boleros for the Disenchanted and Other Plays is published by Theatre Communications Group, Inc., 520 Eighth Avenue, 24th Floor, New York, NY 10018-4156

The publication of *Boleros for the Disenchanted and Other Plays* by José Rivera, through TCG's Book Program, is made possible in part by the New York State Council on the Arts with the support of Governor Andrew Cuomo and the New York State Legislature.

TCG books are exclusively distributed to the book trade by Consortium Book Sales and Distribution.

LIBRARY OF CONGRESS CATALOGING-IN-PUBLICATION DATA
Rivera, José, 1955–
Boleros for the disenchanted and other plays / José Rivera.—1st ed.
p. cm.
ISBN 978-1-55936-390-7
I. Title.
PS3568.I8294B65   2012
812'.54—dc23   2011049308

Book design, cover design and composition by Lisa Govan
Cover art by Vahe Berberian

First Edition, June 2012

For Sona

Contents

Introduction

by Chay Yew

·)¦(·

A S A CHILD, José Rivera loved to sit at his mother's side and listen to stories of his Puerto Rican ancestors. Sagas of inflamed forbidden passions and family betrayals, yarns of star-crossed lovers and disasters staved off. There was also his grandfather's tale of a conquistador in full regalia, astride a white stallion, rupturing out of the trunk of a tree that the old man climbed as a boy.

"The stories were just outrageous, and they were told totally deadpan. This was my life as a little boy," José recalled. "Most people would separate the two: There's reality here, there's the supernatural there; there's the waking life here, there's dreams over there. In the world of my youth, there wasn't that division. There were elements of the fantastical, of the dream, and these things become interchangeable.

"There were incredible storytellers in my family. Especially my mother—she's dazzling. She can sit down and tell stories for hours without taking a breath. So when I did write, it was always about what people were saying."[1]

José's family still continues to inspire his characters or plays. And these plays vividly capture a significant period in José's personal life.

In this superb collection, José continues to tell dazzling stories for the American theatre. Compared to his oeuvre of magic-realism plays, such as *Marisol, Cloud Tectonics* and *References to Salvador Dalí Make Me Hot* (all required reading and the perfect companion to this anthology), these plays mark a detour in stylistic form, braving new aesthetical explorations from one of the most revered American theatre artists. All this attests to José's appetite and courage to always experiment artistically. An original, he's never content to write the familiar in the familiar.

If there is any commonality among the plays in this volume, it is José's investigation of love, marriage and home. All four plays brim with these ideas, and each play eloquently explores them with precision and passion, and in a voice that belongs only to José.

Boleros for the Disenchanted is José's fine tribute to his mother and her long marriage. The first act of the play is set in Miraflores, Puerto Rico, in 1953, where we follow the blossoming romance between Flora and Eusebio. In Act Two, we leap forty years into the future where we find our now married lovers in a small town in Alabama, where an elderly Flora takes care of a bedridden Eusebio suffering from diabetes.

José said, "The idea of *Boleros* is to examine a long-term relationship and how the love you feel for somebody is severely tested when life throws obstacles and tragedies in your way. I literally thought about this play for ten years, wondered about it, and daydreamed about it. Almost all of my work is inspired by something deeply personal, coupled with the larger social and political forces around me. Writing about Puerto Rico was liberating because I was born in Puerto Rico but I left the island when I was four years old."[2]

Perhaps the speech that best captures this heart-wrenching, haunting portrait of love and marriage is when elderly Eusebio counsels a young couple: "This woman, this industrious, indestructible woman stays with me, bathes me and wipes my shit every day without a break." And, "If you can't imagine yourself doing this for someone else, if you can't get your hands dirty, if you can't stand the smell or the pity or the pain in the other person's face, if you'd rather be anywhere else, then you're not ready to be married, my young friends. Call it off. Because it's this or it's nothing."

A play about unconditional love and marriage, *Boleros* is the most naturalistic play in this volume. But it is also a brutal study of transplantation and immigration. In escaping the poverty of the "island of tears," as José has described Puerto Rico, the couple leaves their family and home to make a new life in the United States. There they face a more grueling life as second-class citizens. Yet, as José shows, it is always love that overcomes the loneliness, struggles and disappointments of this new country.

Adoration of the Old Woman is a beautiful and powerful play that deals poignantly with identity. It is also a searing political debate (it is the most political play in this anthology) on the complex history, colonialism and issues of statehood for Puerto Rico. It takes place in a small village in the near future of Puerto Rico, where yet another vote on whether to seek independence or statehood is about to take place. Vanessa, a young Puerto Rican woman from New Jersey, has been sent to stay with her great-grandmother (who is somewhere "between a hundred and a hundred and fifty years old"), Doña Belén, as punishment by her parents.

Once there, Vanessa is courted both sexually and politically by two local men—one representing the pro-independence movement, the other pro-statehood, while Doña Belén engages in hot and scabrous arguments with Adoración, the ghost of her long-dead husband's lover, who is haunting her bed.

When asked why José was interested in writing a play about Puerto Rico, he replied, "When they asked Socrates why health is important, his answer was, 'It's obvious why health is important; you don't have to ask the question.' For me, independence is like that. Puerto Rico is one of the last remaining places in the world that isn't its own country."[3]

In the exquisite short play, *Pablo and Andrew at the Altar of Words*, a Latino/Caucasian gay couple exchange their written wedding vows in front of their family and friends, to, "Say a lot about the kind of love we want to express to each other." And to, "Say the things we never really say in this hugely titantic struggle it can sometimes be just to survive, day to day." In our present age when the right to gay marriage is bitterly fought about, *Pablo and Andrew* is a wise play, the perfect antidote. It celebrates and serves as a testament to the importance of marriage vows that anyone—gay or straight—would value. As Andrew says, "If marriage is about love, why would we want to reduce the amount of love in the world?"

Surreal and terrifyingly potent, *Brainpeople* takes place in a posh apartment in a postapocalyptic, dystopian, militant Los Angeles, under martial law. It centers on Mayannah, a lonely heiress, who, with the promise of money, has invited two desperately poor women to dine on freshly slaughtered tiger flesh. As the evening wears on, we see how deeply disconnected all three women are. Trapped and frightened, one of them utters, "Nothing on this earth is as frightening as another human being." Throughout this mysterious dinner, the facades of the psychologically damaged women are painfully peeled away to reveal their inner truths; every one of them desires something and, in true Rivera style, whatever they want (no matter how destructive) gets fulfilled.

When asked to describe *Brainpeople*, José said, "It is a play that tries to examine mental states and a society in dysfunction. Ultimately, it is about love, death and poverty, and how they contribute to madness. At the same time, I wanted to explore the needs of these women and the world that they create."[4] The result is a sinister, deeply sensuous allegory that exposes the desperation of three women as they cope with isolation and violence in an apocalyptic future.

This collection of José Rivera's plays is a treasure and a vital addition to the canon of the American theatre. A unique and poetical voice, he is a fearless playwright who writes unflinchingly of the beauty and brutality of the human condition, in richly imagined worlds but, also, in worlds in which we live and breathe. He documents us. He warns us. He knows us. He celebrates us. A true poet of the theatre, José Rivera makes us his stories.

Chicago
April 2012

1. Jennifer de Poyen, *San Diego Union-Tribune*, September 22, 2002.
2. Kenneth Jones, Playbill.com, April 7, 2009.
3. de Poyen.
4. Ernio Hernandez, Playbill.com, January 30, 2008.

Chay Yew is a playwright and director. He is Artistic Director of Victory Gardens Theater in Chicago.

Boleros
for the
Disenchanted

•)╪(•

Production History

In 2008 *Boleros for the Disenchanted* received its world premiere at Yale Repertory Theatre in New Haven (James Bundy, Artistic Director; Victoria Nolan, Managing Director). It was directed by Henry Godinez. Linda Buchanan was the set designer. Yuri Cataldo was the costume designer. Joe Appelt was the lighting designer. Veronika Vorel was the sound designer. The stage manager was Danielle Federico. The cast was as follows:

FLORA/EVE	Sona Tatoyan
DOÑA MILLA/OLDER FLORA	Adriana Sevan
DON FERMÍN/OLDER EUSEBIO	Gary Perez
MANUELO/PRIEST	Felix Solis
PETRA/MONICA	Lucia Brawley
EUSEBIO/OSKAR	Joe Minoso

In 2009 *Boleros for the Disenchanted* was produced at American Conservatory Theater in San Francisco (Carey Perloff, Artistic Director; Heather M. Kitchen, Executive Director). It was directed by Carey Perloff. Ralph Funicello was the set designer. Sandra Woodall was the costume designer. Nancy Schertler was the lighting designer. Fabian Obispo was the sound designer and composed original music. Elisa Guthertz was the stage manager. The cast was as follows:

FLORA/EVE	Lela Loren
DOÑA MILLA/OLDER FLORA	Rachel Ticotin
DON FERMÍN/OLDER EUSEBIO	Robert Beltran
MANUELO/OSKAR	Dion Mucciacito
PETRA/MONICA	Michele Vazquez
EUSEBIO/PRIEST	Drew Cortese

In 2009 *Boleros for the Disenchanted* was also produced at the Goodman Theater in Chicago (Robert Falls, Artistic Director; Roche Schulfer, Executive Director). It was directed by Henry Godinez. Linda Buchanan was the set designer. Rachel Anne Healy was the costume designer. Joseph Appelt was the lighting designer. Ray Nardelli and Joshua Horvath were the sound designers. Gustavo Leone was the composer. Alden Vasquez was the production stage manager. The cast was as follows:

FLORA/EVE	Elizabeth Ledo
DOÑA MILLA/OLDER FLORA	Sandra Marquez
DON FERMÍN/OLDER EUSEBIO	René Rivera
MANUELO/PRIEST	Felix Solis
PETRA/MONICA	Liza Fernandez
EUSEBIO/OSKAR	Joe Minoso

CHARACTERS

FLORA, twenty-two

DOÑA MILLA, her mother, forties

DON FERMÍN, her father, fifty-five

MANUELO, her fiancé, thirty

PETRA, her cousin, twenty-one

EUSEBIO, a member of the national guard, twenty-seven

OLDER FLORA, sixty-one

OLDER EUSEBIO, sixty-six

OSKAR, an army private, twenty-seven

MONICA, Oskar's girlfriend, twenty-three

EVE, a nurse, twenty-five

PRIEST

SETTING

1953 in Miraflores, Puerto Rico.
1992 in Daleville, Alabama.

Note

The actors may be doubled as follows:

FLORA/EVE

DOÑA MILLA/OLDER FLORA

DON FERMÍN/OLDER EUSEBIO

MANUELO/PRIEST

PETRA/MONICA

EUSEBIO/OSKAR

Act One

·)|(·

Scene 1

1953.

Miraflores, Puerto Rico, a tiny hamlet of small, poor, brightly painted, wood-and-concrete houses with porches and pretty gardens.

The surrounding land is green, generous, dense, fecund; a presence.

Front yard of Flora's house. Several old chairs and a little table on the porch. The garden is filled with bright, tangled wildflowers and herbs. It extends downstage to a narrow dirt road, which connects it to the barrio's other houses.

Coquís chirp. A large moon looms on this cool, breezy night.

The front door opens and Flora enters, crying.

She is twenty-two, thin, a childhood victim of rickets, long black hair, green eyes, pale skin with beauty marks, a serious, pious girl. She goes across the porch to the garden.

MILLA'S VOICE: Flora!

(The front door opens again and Doña Milla, Flora's mother, forties, a strong, unschooled and earthy woman, enters. She watches Flora cry from the porch.)

FLORA: I don't believe you! Why would you tell me something like that?

MILLA: Angel, come inside before people see you.

FLORA: Who saw it, Mom? Tell me *who.*

MILLA: She doesn't want me to tell you . . .

FLORA: Then how am I supposed to believe it? People say stupid things all the time around here! People have nothing better to do than sit around El Quince telling lies about people they don't even know.

(Beat.)

MILLA: It was . . . Doña Marta who saw him first.

FLORA: Doña Marta's half blind!

MILLA: Only in one eye!

FLORA: And she's crazy. She hears voices. Sees ghosts. She is completely unreliable and I'm glad you told me because now I know it's all a mistake and—

MILLA: Don Tomás saw him, too.

FLORA *(Beat, realizing)*: He's got really good eyesight . . .

MILLA: It's cold out here. Come inside, go to bed and we'll all have more strength in the—

FLORA: Where did it happen? Don't make me ask you twice.

MILLA: In the plaza in Arecibo.

FLORA: When?

MILLA: Monday. Tuesday also. And he was spotted on Wednesday through Friday.

FLORA: And they're sure, absolutely *sure*, it's *my* Manuelo they saw with that woman?

MILLA: These people are our friends, Flora, why would they lie?

(Flora starts to cry.

Doña Milla goes to the garden and holds Flora, who cries into her chest.)

FLORA: I just want to die, Mami.

MILLA: Don't say those sinful things, my darling.

FLORA: But I don't know why I'm being punished like this.

MILLA: We never know why, my angel . . . all we know is that the pain we feel is unbearable. But then we wake up one day and realize it wasn't a punishment after all, it was actually a blessing. That God did not abandon you but loved you more than ever. And what He was really doing was *testing* you. And when it mattered most, you were strong and passed His test with flying colors.

FLORA: I'm going to kill Manuelo. I'm really going to hurt him. And he's going to beg me to stop hurting him and I'll stop and he'll realize what a prize I am, how lucky he is to even know my name, then he's going to want me back and he'll repent and ask my forgiveness and I'll withhold it for a while—a *long while*—and it'll drive him crazy and he'll be on the verge of losing his mind and maybe even *killing* himself (which I'll be secretly enjoying) . . . and then I'll forgive him and take him back and we'll get married like we're supposed to and have the most beautiful children.

MILLA: All that, huh?

FLORA: I'm just warming up. When I get through with him, he's going to wish he was never born.

MILLA: What a happy couple you two are going to be.

FLORA: You think so?

(Off her look.)

I'm serious! I know I'm young. But I take this seriously. It's a commitment before God, Christ and the Mother of God.

MILLA: That matters less, angel, than knowing this is a commitment you make *to each other*. To your own heart. Which is fragile and must be protected.

FLORA: I understand that.

MILLA: Do you? Have you really thought about this? Are you sure Manuelo's the one? The absolute one?

FLORA: Yes. It is written. By God himself. In big burning letters.

MILLA *(Tries not to laugh)*: Okay then. Burning letters!

FLORA: The hottest fire there is.

MILLA: Because marriage isn't all laughter, parties and making babies. Marriage is hell on earth if you're not happy. If you feel trapped and all he does is waste his time with other women and drink . . . and then it's a hundred times worse if he hits you—and they do—even the sweetest, most loving boy . . . when he's angry and he's got a little rum in him and you haven't made love in a while and there's no one else to blame for his problems and failures—*pow*—a fist between the eyes. I've seen it a million times, young lady.

FLORA: Manuelo would never.

MILLA: I was like you: I thought I was so sure and I didn't know him very long and he was all smiles and flattery and it looked like a long happy life without tears. And I was wrong.

FLORA: But you love Papi.

MILLA: Of course I love him. The way Jesus loved his cross. Because there's no choice but to love. Because you two are *in* it and there's no changing fate, you *endure*, and even in this seeming holocaust there's still a little drop of love.

FLORA: You're not planning on speaking at the wedding, are you?

MILLA: Boba! There's not going to be a wedding until you and Manuelo sit down like two serious people and get to the truth.

FLORA: Yes. That's what we have to do. Right away.

MILLA: Don't let him sweet-talk you. Look in his eyes. The mouth will lie but the soul *knows*. And if you're smart and look deep into his soul, you'll know, too.

(Beat. Trying not to cry.)

You are . . . my Flora . . . I don't want to see you hurt anymore.

FLORA: Oh, Mami, you know I love you so much . . .

*(Flora goes to embrace Doña Milla and is interrupted by the
appearance of Flora's father, Don Fermín, a small man, like
a bantam chicken, tough as nails, dark and weathered by
the sun, ramrod straight despite his fifty-five years. He's very
drunk.)*

FERMÍN: What are you two idiots doing out at night?

FLORA: Papi, we're just talking.

FERMÍN: Was I talking to you?

FLORA: No, Papi.

MILLA: We're just out here talking, Moncho.

FERMÍN: For the whole world to see? Two ignorant jíbaras, out in
the night, gossiping, wasting time and looking like fools? For
what? So everyone can laugh at us?

MILLA: Everyone's in bed by this time.

FERMÍN: Except my two whores! Get inside, for the love of God!
What do you think this is?

FLORA *(Soft)*: Mami is not a whore.

FERMÍN: What did you say?

MILLA: Flora, just get in—

FERMÍN: No, I want to hear—

FLORA: I said Mami is not a whore. Mami is a saint. And you
should be kissing her feet not calling her—!

(Don Fermín slaps Flora across the face.)

FERMÍN: For the love of Jesus, who do you think you are?

MILLA: Moncho! Don't touch her!

*(Don Fermín goes to slap Flora again but Doña Milla gets
between them.)*

FLORA: And Mami did not raise a whore, as God is my witness!

FERMÍN: You hear the disrespect?

FLORA: You're the one who disrespects!

FERMÍN: The faster you're married the better!

FLORA: You can say that again!

FERMÍN: I hope Manuelo disciplines you and teaches you respect and slaps you so hard your teeth fall out of your head.

FLORA: It'll still be better than living with you!

MILLA: Flora—what are you *saying*?

(Don Fermín drunkenly attempts to take off his belt.)

FERMÍN: In my father's time, such talk was treated as it should.

MILLA *(To Flora)*: Inside *now*.

FLORA: I'm not going to leave you alone with him.

MILLA: I've been handling him for twenty-five years! *Inside*, girl!

(Don Fermín gets his belt off, swings it at the women, but misses. Laughs.)

FERMÍN: You're the biggest fool I know. Marrying that asshole. He's had half the girls in Miraflores . . . only an idiot like you would be happy with a man like that. You should hear what they're saying at El Quince!

MILLA: Put the belt down, Moncho.

FERMÍN: Not until she learns the meaning of respect. In my time we knew what that was. It was everything.

(Don Fermín stops waving the belt and is suddenly very still, deeply sad.)

We were men back then. We had land. We were never paid much but we worked hard. And we came home to children who were put on this earth to make us happy.

(Doña Milla cautiously goes to Don Fermín and takes the belt.)

MILLA: That was an old time, Monchito. Not today.

FERMÍN: Today . . . they pay a man to do nothing, so he does nothing. Today children talk back and don't understand the sacrifices you make, or why it's important to treat a man like the king he is.

MILLA *(Holding him)*: It's a new world, my love.

FERMÍN: And we lost our work, so we lost our purpose in this world of pain, this purgatory, this garden of snakes and disease! Strip a man of work, his balls shrivel like he's castrated. The American mafias walk in because we don't have the balls to stop them and what do we do instead? We drink and scream like fools and come home at night to whip and insult our own beloved women.

(Doña Milla holds Don Fermín and motions Flora to join them. She doesn't want to but does it anyway.)

MILLA *(Softly, to Flora)*: Thank you, my angel.

FERMÍN *(To Flora)*: Ask for my blessings.

FLORA: May I have your blessings, Papi?

FERMÍN: May the Lord keep you and bless you, my sweet beauty.

FLORA: Thank you, Papi.

FERMÍN: Look at you. So grown up. May God give you nine children and long nights of happiness and may you not disappoint your man or bring disgrace to our name, you understand?

FLORA: I'll do my best, Papi.

MILLA *(To Don Fermín)*: Just put your belt on before your pants fall off and you bring disgrace to all of Miraflores.

FERMÍN *(Putting on his belt)*: Ha! I'm hungry. Is there anything to eat around here?

MILLA: That's the most insulting thing you've said all night. There's always something to eat in this house.

FERMÍN: Heat it up. Bring me a plate full of happiness.

(Don Fermín, trying to get his belt on, stumbles to the house.)

Look at this land. The richest on earth. Spit in the ground, a tree grows. Reach into any branch and feed yourself with the thickest, sweetest fruit. Now, we send our food up north for next to nothing . . . and it comes back to us in expensive tin cans. And every day the best and brightest get on airplanes to starve and freeze in New York until you have no family left to keep you sane and loved. Yes. Get married, Flora. Bring more children into this hell.

(Don Fermín exits into the house.
  Flora and Doña Milla look at each other. Lights to black.)

Scene 2

A few days later.

Doña Milla, in the garden, pulls up medicinal herbs, talks to the flowers.

MILLA: What's wrong with you? I give you love every day and you still look like shit. *(To another plant)* You! I'm not even talking to you! No! Don't give me that look!

(As she picks herbs, a young man of thirty approaches, wearing a cotton suit, slender and handsome, a pencil-thin mustache: Manuelo.

Manuelo tries to play it cool but he is scared to death of Doña Milla.)

MANUELO: Doña Milla.
MILLA: Ah. Manuelo.
MANUELO: Will you bless me?

MILLA: God bless you.
MANUELO: Thank you.

(Beat.)

The garden.
MILLA: Plants. Herbs.
MANUELO: Growing so fast!
MILLA: It's shit. Something's wrong with the soil. You used to see these plants grow up to here. Now you have to pull them by the ears to make them grow. What are you doing?
MANUELO: Walking to your house.
MILLA: What's at my house?
MANUELO: I heard that Flora . . .
MILLA: My *daughter* Flora!
MANUELO: Yes, your daughter—
MILLA: The one you're engaged to!
MANUELO: Yes. That she wanted to see me—
MILLA: You know she's my only daughter?
MANUELO: Yes, Doña Milla, I was aware.
MILLA: You know that my only son is gone?
MANUELO: I know that too—
MILLA: Efraín got into a fight with his father. Over something I don't even remember. Moncho grabbed his hair, knocked him down, kicked his face, his ribs, we begged him to stop, but once Moncho gets started . . . mouth bleeding, Efraín spits out a tooth and punches the wall—puts a hole in it, that's how strong he is. He runs out of the house and we never see him again. Now—there are rumors of him in the Bronx. Fixing cars. Playing his guitar. Loving the girls. He doesn't write or visit, like we don't exist. Like we're ghosts.
MANUELO: You've told me this story on several occasions.
MILLA: Yes, I repeat it a lot, especially to you, do you know why?
MANUELO: No, Doña Milla, I don't really know.
MILLA: Because I have no sisters. My brothers have six daughters and all of them left for the United States. Flora stayed. If you

16

break her heart—the only child we have left—who loves and respects us and will be a virgin on her wedding night and has never sinned and has the cleanest reputation in Miraflores—ask anybody—if you break this young woman's heart, I will castrate you with a rusty machete under a full moon, you understand me, my Manuelo?

MANUELO: Yes, it's very clear, Doña Milla.

MILLA: Good. *(Calling)* Flora! The love of your life is here! The man who will soon swear unconditional love in front of his family, your family, God, the President of the USA, and abuelo's machete!

(Flora appears at the door. She's in her best dress, makeup on; she manages to look innocent and sexy, vulnerable and feisty.)

FLORA: Oh, look, Manuelo's here.

MILLA: What are you wearing?!

FLORA: Mami, do you think you should get Manuelo a cup of coffee?

MANUELO: But coffee gives me gas—

FLORA: Get Manuelo a hot cup of coffee, Mami, a big one.

MILLA: Makeup? In the middle of the day?

(Off Flora's look:)

Yes, coffee. Coming right up.

(Doña Milla goes into the house.
Flora and Manuelo look at each other awkwardly.)

MANUELO: Your mother talks to plants.

(Beat. Flora just stares at him.)

I heard about this thing called television?

(Beat.)

. . . Like the suit?

FLORA: The Bible condemns liars, Manuelo.

MANUELO: Do you want to take a walk?

FLORA: Anything we say, we can say in the sanctity of my home.

MANUELO: Is Don Fermín home?

FLORA: Why are you so afraid of my father?

MANUELO: Because your parents have this unnerving tendency to threaten to remove my balls.

FLORA *(Laughs)*: I can't believe you said that word! Oh God, I'm going to pee-pee!

MANUELO: Honey, please, can we go?

FLORA: Papi's not home. You're relatively safe. Come closer to me.

(Manuelo reluctantly comes up to the porch.)

MANUELO: Okay.

FLORA: Kiss me lightly on the cheek.

(He does so.
Flora motions him to sit. They sit.
Doña Milla comes out with a hot cup of coffee. She hands it to Manuelo.)

MANUELO: A million thanks, Doña Milla. Smells good.

MILLA: We used to grow our own coffee in the hills of Utuado and Adjuntas . . .

FLORA *(Has heard it a million times)*: . . . now we buy it from America for exorbitant prices. Mami? Please?

MILLA: It's not right to leave you young people alone.

FLORA: We're engaged. I'm sure the Holy Ghost will understand.

MILLA: It's not the Holy Ghost I worry about, it's our neighbors—

(Flora stamps her foot.)

I'll be inside. The door stays open.

(Doña Milla exits into the house. The door stays open. We see her on a rocking chair, listening to the conversation.
Awkward silence.)

MANUELO: They say that television will be able to bring you pictures from all over the world. If I had two extra nickels to rub together I'd invest in it—

FLORA: Are you sleeping with Sylvia Cárdenas?

MANUELO: No. Absolutely not. On my life, my mother's life, the souls of my ancestors, I have never touched Sylvia Cárdenas.

FLORA: I knew that. I wanted to see what your face looks like when you're telling the truth. Then who is she, Manuelo?

MANUELO: Where do you—how can you talk to me like—?

FLORA: Look, I don't want to be talking to you like this. I don't like these feelings I have right now. So please, be the man I think you are, and just tell me the truth, I can handle it, but I cannot handle lies and silences, ever, not from any person, but least of all from the only man I've ever loved, the only man who's hand I've touched, the man who used to make me wake up smiling and singing and—

MANUELO: I did it with Adriana Rodríguez.

(Flora bursts into tears.)

FLORA: How can you say that to me?! How can you be so cruel?!

MANUELO: You asked me her name!

FLORA: I asked you to tell me all the gossip was untrue! I asked you to confirm for me that you were an honest, faithful man that really loved me! I didn't ask you to blurt out a name! Adriana Rodríguez, Adriana Rodríguez! *I shit on Adriana Rodríguez!*

(Doña Milla gasps out loud.
  Even Manuelo is stunned.)

MANUELO: Flora Dolores Encarnación!

FLORA: Oh shut up! Don't say her name and then say my name with your ugly, dirty mouth!

(Flora cries.
  Manuelo wipes his brow nervously.)

MANUELO: God, please don't do that.

FLORA: Why? Because it makes you *sad*? Because you feel guilty for stabbing me in the heart? Oh, poor Manuelo!

MANUELO: I still care about you . . .

FLORA: Do you do it with her all the time? Where do you go? This whole town is full of spies. If you take a shit in the morning, half the town knows and they're gossiping about it to the other half that afternoon!

MANUELO: That's not important, Flora.

FLORA: When was the last time you did it with her? Last night? This morning? Ten minutes ago? Don't touch me with those dirty hands! I bet you haven't even washed since then!

(Sniffs him.)

Is that what sin smells like, Manuelo? Is that the stink of faithlessness?

MANUELO: You're getting hysterical.

FLORA: And you're getting castrated!

MILLA: Amen!

MANUELO: Flora, come on, for the love of God, people can hear you, it's undignified.

(Flora stands. Shouts to the neighborhood.)

FLORA: The rumors are true! Manuelo Ramón Delgado is a cheat!

(Manuelo pushes Flora back into her chair, rougher than he intended.)

MANUELO: That's enough of that. You're acting like a child. Like a little jíbara who doesn't know how the world is.

FLORA *(Truly furious)*: You dare lecture me? You're lucky my brother and my father are not here.

MANUELO: Yes, I'll lecture you, because your parents keep you in the dark about life in general and men specifically.

(Doña Milla approaches the door.)

MILLA: Wait one minute.

MANUELO: Doña Milla this is between your daughter and myself and I am telling you to stay in that house. I am telling you that!

(Doña Milla, taken aback by his tone, stops in her tracks.)

FLORA: He's finally right about something, Mami, stay inside.

(Doña Milla sits back down.
   Manuelo paces across the porch.)

MANUELO: God made men and women differently, Flora. That's the first thing you need to know. I didn't make this difference between man and woman, God did—and I have inherited those differences. I cannot control them. A man is, basically, despite language, culture, religion and the invention of television, a creature of instinct, like a dog. We are controlled by such desperate forces, Flora, such demonic energy . . . I just hope you never experience them yourself. They make a man do crazy things. Things that are repulsive and wrong—but, here's the catch: *things that must be done.* Yes, Flora. A man *must* sin. It's in our blood. It's innate and natural and it is a command of our bestial selves. A man must be with a woman. There I said it. And God, in his infinite flexibility, has created certain special women for men like me to be with. These are not the chaste virgins of his acquaintance: his sisters, cousins, novias. No, these girls are *other* men's sisters, cousins and novias. They are built with the special purpose of fulfilling nature's special plan for men like me. So we don't dirty women like you. So you can stay pure, closer to God and the Holy Spirit. Flora, come on. Do you ask a tiger not to stalk the antelope? Do you ask the fish not to, to, to do what fish do all day? No. You let nature *be.* You let the rain fall. You let the flower blossom. And you must let a man be a man, Flora. I have waited a year for you. A man cannot stop being a man for a year. *That's* sin. And our engagement is for yet another year. Two years in which my flower will not blossom! Is that fair? Because in those two years, you continue to be a woman. You clean for your father, you cook for him, obey him, you learn from his wisdom. You fulfill the strict destiny penned by God for womanhood. You get to be you. So why shouldn't I get to be I? Or me? Whoever Manuelo Ramón Delgado really is? You see, I'm just trying to be fair here.

FLORA: Fair.

MANUELO: Flora, there is love. And there is sex. And they are two different things. The love I feel for you is inexpressible. It's bigger and deeper than the oceans that encircle this whole earth with their oceanic bigness and deepness. No! That's wrong! That's poorly said, Manuelo! I love you to my dying breath, Flora. I love you in truth, in trust, in holiness, in sin, in pleasure, in family, in wonder, in God's presence, in all my capacity and imagination. I love you like the page loves the pen that writes the eternal words "I love you" on its white, pure skin. Believe me, Flora, please.

FLORA: I want to. Because I love you, Man—

MANUELO: I feel that love, every time I see you. It's a heat, an energy, and I forget where I am or what time it is or what's up or down.

FLORA: I've never loved like this—

MANUELO: And don't you know how lucky I feel? Of all the men walking this sad earth, I was the chosen one! Little old Manuelo Ramón Delgado. Loved like no other man by a woman who is like no other woman.

FLORA: I'd make the perfect wife—

MANUELO: And mother! Can't you see them, Flora, scampering around the house, little noses running, you tuck them in at night and sing them to peaceful sleep.

FLORA: I would kill for you because that's the way I love. I don't do anything halfway—

MANUELO: And who knows better than—?

FLORA: —*Don't interrupt me again.* I have a nature too, Manuelo. And it's capable of a love so great . . . I have no words for it. Because a mystery like love cannot be explained. Only felt. And the love I feel for you is blue like infinite sky, red like a volcano's heart, pure like all the water that surrounds Puerto Rico.

MANUELO: Yes. *Completely.*

FLORA: And it's a love that needs to be, I hope you're listening, respected. And treated fairly. Which means: what I give when I love, that's what I expect in return. Nothing more or less, Manuelo.

MANUELO: Of course, dear . . .

FLORA: And I give complete, unquestioned, life-long fidelity. That's a promise to God. Made on my mother's eyes. And that's what I expect from you.

MANUELO: Well, yes, yes, my love, once we're married . . .

FLORA: No. Not "once we're married." I want this fidelity from you today. And tonight. For the three-hundred-sixty-five days and nights left, you turn your back on the Adriana Rodríguezes of Puerto Rico.

MANUELO: But I just told you, given my nature, it's impossible—

FLORA: Tame your nature. Overcome the animal inside you. The dog. Put it on a damn leash.

MANUELO: Easier said than done!

FLORA: Manuelo, when you go to a store to buy a diamond, do they just give it to you? No. You pay something for it. Am I a diamond of a girl or not?

MANUELO: Of, of course you are.

FLORA: I don't ask you to be governor of Puerto Rico. I don't ask for a nice house or a car or even a television, whatever the hell that is. I ask that you don't put your thing inside another girl's thing from now until the day one of us dies. After that I don't care where you stick it. That's what this diamond costs.

MANUELO: And you're saying you can't be flexible?

FLORA: Do I look flexible?

MANUELO: Why do you have to be so goddamn stubborn? Why can't you look the other way and see me as human? Why can't you forgive a little weakness? Why does everything have to be *absolute* for you?

FLORA: Because it does.

MANUELO: The word for that is *hubris*, Flora, and hubris is always punished by the gods. It's sad, and I feel sorry for you.

FLORA: So you're saying you won't hold out for me?

MANUELO: You're asking me the impossible! Go to any person in Miraflores and explain this situation and they will laugh in your face, Flora! You expect to marry a man but you won't let him be a man? What kind of woman are you?

FLORA *(Trying not to cry)*: I can't believe you're doing this to me . . .

MANUELO: Refusing to let you control me? How is that bad?

FLORA: Breaking my heart is what's bad!

MANUELO: If you can't tame your jealousy and possessiveness and desire to control my entire life *you're* bad!

FLORA: Get off my porch!

MANUELO: This is on *you*, Flora. You sacrifice marriage to a really great guy because you're stubborn. I am a catch. I am the best this stink-hole town has to offer. But you'll turn your nose up at me. You. The only one stupid enough to do that!

FLORA *(Crying)*: Just go.

MANUELO: Cry. Be weak. Be the little nothing you are. I can't wait to tell this story at El Quince. What a good, long laugh this town's going to have at your expense!

FLORA: Mami, tell him to go!

*(Doña Milla appears at the doorway.
Manuelo turns to her.)*

MANUELO: What kind of mother lets a girl grow as old as Flora without teaching her the facts of life?

FLORA *(Crying, to Manuelo)*: You're so ugly to me right now.

MILLA: Manuelo Ramón Delgado, I must ask you to never call on Flora again.

MANUELO: Talk to her, Doña Milla. Make her understand that she is never going to find a man as good as me. Not some little, skinny, cross-eyed idiot like her!

(Flora stands, trembling, takes off her engagement ring, crosses to Manuel and thrusts the ring in his hand.)

FLORA: Take this. And take to bed all the whores you want. Because that's all you deserve. The caresses and poetry and honor and disease and cruelty of a whore's immaculate love. A real man would never be satisfied with the sad pleasure between a whore's legs—but it's good enough for you. No—it's better than you can expect in this life, you vain, hypocritical, dirty, little eunuch!

(Flora runs into the house, crying, slams the door behind her. Doña Milla can't look at Manuelo, who can't look at her.)

MANUELO: You raised a fool.

(Lights to black.)

Scene 3

That night. A gentle darkness.

On the porch, Flora tries to concentrate on the domino game she plays with Don Fermín as Doña Milla looks on. Don Fermín is a much sweeter man sober.

FERMÍN *(As pleasant as can be)*: I can have him killed, you know.

FLORA: Yeah, that'll solve everything, Papi.

FERMÍN: I wouldn't even have to pay. On my word alone, wheels will turn, justice will be done. And it's so clean, it'll never get traced back to you.

FLORA: Me? I don't want a murder on my conscience! Don't you think I've suffered enough? In my mind, he no longer exists.

MILLA: And the pain in your soul? Back when I was a girl, men died for less.

FERMÍN: Men died if they *looked* at a girl the wrong way. The Spanish may have been barbarians, but they at least brought to this

26

island the concept of honor. That's what the American mafia has stripped from us. They've raped our sense of honor up the ass!

FLORA: The Yanquis didn't make Manuelo do what he—

FERMÍN: Before we were dismembered by all the immigration, the most important thing was a man's honor. Now? Any asshole can commit any indiscretion and he doesn't worry about the community's disapproval because the next morning he's on a plane to LaGuardia! And when these people get sick of being exploited and worshipping the dollar, they come back to the island and bring all the vice, greed, abuse and lack of manners they learned in Bayonne and Patterson with them. What does that do to a community? All this leaving and coming back, leaving and coming back? Forgetting the old ways and bringing in new contamination? Where does honor go after that?

MILLA: Down the toilet.

FERMÍN: Completely down the toilet.

FLORA: You two are so good at cheering me up.

FERMÍN: I know why you don't like murder. It's messy. You think it's going to happen with a gun, or someone's going to open his head with a machete. I'm much too subtle for that! You remember Don Faustino, don't you? How did he die?

FLORA: Cancer of the stomach.

FERMÍN *(Laughs)*: Cancer of the stomach!

MILLA *(Laughs)*: Cancer of the stomach!

FLORA: How is that funny?

FERMÍN: Angel—you are so innocent. You remember what happened just before he got this "cancer of the stomach"? His chickens got into my beans and ate them all and he wouldn't fix the fence and I kept losing beans like a pendejo.

FLORA: You didn't poison him, did you?

FERMÍN: Who has money for poison? I did what my father would've done. I went to Doña Felicia.

FLORA: The witch?

MILLA: She put a spell on Don Faustino . . . and he was dead in six months. Nice, huh?

FLORA: But—how do you know he wasn't sick already? And he would've died anyway?

MILLA: Atheist. You sure you're not a gringa?

FLORA (Crossing herself): I don't want to believe that stuff. It scares me.

MILLA: That's too bad because . . . well, I paid a visit to Doña Felicia today . . . and she told me it's no problem for you to get Manuelo back. She knows a spell that'll make him faithful to you for the rest of your life.

FERMÍN: And she isn't even going to charge us! All she asks for is a few dozen pasteles and that you name the first girl after her.

FLORA: Mami, and Papi, I'll say this one time only: if I can't keep Manuelo, or any man, on the strength of my love, I don't want him through magic. If my love isn't magic enough . . .

(Tearing up.)

. . . I wasn't going to cry anymore! Oh my God, I'm losing my mind!

(Flora moves away from her parents as she struggles to control her crying.)

FERMÍN: Goddamn him! Goddamn that boy!

MILLA (Going to Flora): Honey . . .

FLORA: No, I'm not going to murder Manuelo or enchant him into falling in love with me. I have to look to myself and figure out what's so wrong with me that a man would rather chase a whore.

MILLA: What he did is not your fault!

FLORA: If I were plumper or prettier or liked to drink and laugh at dirty jokes or if I was just a little more *fun*, he would have never—

MILLA: Nonsense. If Manuelo married Cleopatra, he'd cheat.

FLORA: I don't have enough magic to keep a man. Twenty-two and I'm never going to be married. And I've been so conceited.

God is punishing me for that. So many nice boys liked me and I didn't like them because one was too short, or another had no teeth, or another had a crooked back and two wives in Mayagüez! The word for that is hubris!

(Doña Milla holds Flora. Doña Milla and Don Fermín make eye contact, silent communication between them.)

MILLA: This is not going to change Manuelo or heal the pain . . . but I think you need to go away a while. To some place where everything isn't going to remind you of Manuelo.
FLORA *(Looks at Doña Milla)*: Where? The moon?
MILLA: Why don't you go be with your cousin Petra in Santurce?
FLORA: Petra? I would love that! Petra would understand! Are you serious? Papi, are you okay with this?
FERMÍN: I think this is an emergency and just this once I can allow it.
FLORA: Oh my God. The great city of Santurce.
MILLA: Just for a month or so. You're not going to spend the rest of your life there, God forbid.
FLORA: And Petra! Oh, thank you, Mami!

(Hugs her.)

Thank you, Papi!

(Hugs him.)

I will work so hard to forget Manuelo. When I come back, he will be erased from my memory and stricken from my heart. And I will be completely free, I promise.

(Lights to black.)

Scene 4

Several weeks later. A hot night.

A street corner in Santurce. On one side of a narrow alleyway is the entrance to an apartment building. On the adjacent corner is a grocery store with a jukebox near the entrance.

Flora and her pretty cousin, Petra, twenty-one, leave the grocery store, licking ice-cream cones. They cross the alleyway and sit on a bench in front of the apartment building.

PETRA: I'm *definitely* going to the U.S. There's no way they're going to keep me here. Get married, stay in this apartment the rest of my life? Raise a dozen kids and waste away at forty? How's that ice cream?

FLORA *(Barely listening)*: It's okay.

PETRA: I see what happens to girls our age, married to frustrated men who can't find a job, they try a little while, but no one's got unlimited patience. They sit around the house, drink beer, listen to the radio, get bored. Then they go out with their friends, drink some more and when they come home—forget it. War! How's that ice cream?

FLORA: I told you—good.

PETRA: I just want to make sure you were still alive.

FLORA: I'm listening. You hate it here.

PETRA: I hate what it's *become*. I want better. You ever think of leaving?

FLORA: Sometimes. When Papi hits me. When I see what Mami's life is like. But then . . . I remember how much I love the island.

PETRA: Because it's all you know.

FLORA: I know as much as you. You've never been anywhere.

PETRA: But I have this little thing you don't: it's called imagination.

FLORA: You're a dreamer, Petra. I'm trying to be practical.

PETRA: It's not practical to stay on this island: it's suicidal.

FLORA: But I hear such terrible things about up there. Cold winter, criminals with drugs and guns, terrible poverty, violence, racist police, everything's super expensive, no one talks to each other, no one believes in God. How can anybody live in a place with atomic bombs? That's a sin! They burn you alive!

PETRA: You read too much.

FLORA: What have you heard from your own brother? Doesn't he tell you how scared he is up there? The whites don't want him, the black people don't. Has he found a job yet? A good church?

PETRA: My brother would be unhappy in Paradise. And all those things—drugs, guns, poverty—they're here in Santurce, too. Or take a walk through La Perla. All cities are bad. That's why, when I move to the United States, I'm going to the countryside and grow beans and have chickens and lots of open space. Not every Puerto Rican has to move to the Bronx. That's stupid. It's a big, big country. We could move anywhere, Flora.

FLORA *(Hadn't thought of that)*: It is a big country. Should we go inside? It's not right to be out like this.

PETRA: What a jíbara! You're not in the dumb little town. It's the city, girl, it's 1953, live a little, okay? Besides, it's too hot to go inside.

FLORA: I never felt it so hot. What is God thinking?

(As if to answer Flora's question, Eusebio appears upstage. Eusebio is twenty-seven, medium height, wearing a National Guard uniform, pressed khaki pants, carrying a duffle bag. Eusebio is tired from a long walk.

As he approaches the corner where Petra and Flora sit, he notices the jukebox in the grocery store. He stops to put a coin in the machine. The bolero "Dolores" plays.)

PETRA *(Noticing Eusebio)*: Who's that guy?
FLORA: He's playing "Dolores."

(Eusebio smiles as he listens to the song. Puts down the heavy duffle bag. He notices the two young women on the bench and smiles.)

PETRA *(Whispers)*: He smiled at you!
FLORA *(Whispers)*: Who?
PETRA: That guy, stupid! The soldier.
FLORA: No he didn't.
PETRA: You weren't looking.

(Eusebio smiles and nods at the girls.)

(Whispers) He did it again! Jesus! He is fresh!

(Eusebio picks up the duffle bag and crosses the alleyway to their bench.)

EUSEBIO: Hi. That's my favorite song.
PETRA *(Whispers to Flora)*: He's talking to us! *(To Eusebio)* Hi. It's her middle name. Dolores.
EUSEBIO: No kidding. Dolores.
PETRA *(Whispering to Flora)*: It's his favorite song!
FLORA: Yes, I heard him, Petra.
PETRA *(Whispers to Flora)*: He's talking to us! *(To Eusebio)* So, are you in the army?

EUSEBIO: National Guard.

PETRA: Oh. National Guard. Boats and submarines and watery death!

EUSEBIO *(Smiles)*: I missed my bus.

PETRA *(Whispers)*: *He's so cute in that uniform!*

FLORA *(Embarrassed)*: Don't mind my cousin Petra, sir, she's retarded.

EUSEBIO *(Laughs)*: I usually take the bus from the ship to the bar-
racks, but I missed the last one. That's why I'm walking. *(To Flora)* Do you live around here?

PETRA: She lives in Miraflores. You?

EUSEBIO: I'm from Ponce. *(To Flora)* Have you ever been to Ponce?

FLORA: I've never been to Ponce, no.

EUSEBIO: You should go, it's beautiful.

FLORA: I don't need to see Ponce because Miraflores is beautiful.

EUSEBIO *(Can't take his eyes off Flora)*: It must be very beautiful.
My name's Eusebio. What's yours?

FLORA *(Hesitates)*: Well, I don't know if it's proper to tell you—

PETRA: My name is Petra. I live right here in this building. I've been
to Ponce. It's amazing.

EUSEBIO: Did you see the Taino ball courts?

PETRA: I love them. I love everything in Ponce. I love all things Taino.

EUSEBIO *(To Flora)*: So you're just visiting here?

FLORA: That's right, sir.

EUSEBIO: For how long?

FLORA: A month or so.

EUSEBIO: That's a nice long vacation.

FLORA: It's not a vacation, sir.

PETRA: She had her heart mangled by a man. Doesn't trust 'em.

FLORA: Ay, Petra!

EUSEBIO *(Sincere)*: That's too bad. I'm sorry to hear that.

(Beat.)

I'd—I'd like to talk to you again.

FLORA: I don't see how you can. I shouldn't be out here. It's too hot
to be inside. And. I don't know—it's not possible, I'm sorry.

PETRA: Unless you miss your bus again.

EUSEBIO: Yes, I'd have to be unlucky enough to miss my bus again. Do you have a phone number?

PETRA: We do—

FLORA: No. There is no number. You seem like a nice man, but I don't know you, sir, how can I give a complete stranger my number? What kind of girl do you think you're talking to?

EUSEBIO: You're absolutely right.

(Glances at his watch.)

Well, I should go then. You get in trouble if you report to the barracks after curfew, and I don't know these streets. Thank you for listening to that bolero with me. It's my favorite one. Makes me smile.

FLORA: Yes, I like it, too.

EUSEBIO: Ladies, good night.

FLORA: Good night, sir.

PETRA: Bye. See ya later, soldier!

(Eusebio smiles at the pretty girls, picks up his duffle bag and disappears up the street.
  Brief silence as the girls watch him go.)

FLORA: Why do you have to be so crazy!?

PETRA: I'm not the crazy one! It's you, turning your nose up at that very nice piece of meat over there! Look at that ass!

FLORA: Petra, my God, you are going right to hell for that mouth!

PETRA: How can you let him walk away like this?

FLORA: I'm not going to start chasing after men. It's disgusting when girls do that.

PETRA: But wouldn't it be nice to see him again? Maybe he's a good guy. Just because Manuelo was a dick.

FLORA: What am I supposed to do? It was a chance meeting—a freak occurrence—means nothing.

PETRA: You turn it into nothing with that attitude.

FLORA: You think I'm in any position to talk freely to a man? I know he's not Manuelo, but I look at him and all I see is Manuelo. Makes me remember how stupid I was and I don't want to be stupid for a man ever again. Besides, it was you he liked, not me.

PETRA: Oh no, girl, it was definitely you. I could see. That uniform. Those lips. Good old-fashioned Puerto Rican manhood right there.

FLORA: You're embarrassing me, Petra. Let's go inside.

PETRA: I'm going to have some hot dreams tonight, remembering those lips!

(Lights to black.)

Scene 5

Two weeks later. Santurce. Night.

Flora is alone on the bench. She seems to be waiting for something. The jukebox plays a melancholy bolero.

Flora looks down the alleyway. Nothing. She gets up from the bench, goes to the door of the apartment building. Goes inside.

Eusebio enters through the alleyway and disappears into the store.

In a moment, Flora is back outside. She hesitates. Sits on the bench again and waits a moment. Feels foolish. Stands.

EUSEBIO'S VOICE: Hey Miraflores!

> *(Flora recognizes the voice. Rushes to the apartment door.*
> *Eusebio comes out of the grocery store, holding two cans*
> *of beer.)*

EUSEBIO: Miraflores!

(Flora stops at the door. Concludes it's rude to not respond to him.)

FLORA: That's not my name, sir.

EUSEBIO: Miraflores Dolores is not your name?

FLORA: It's—Flora, sir.

EUSEBIO: Yes, it's pretty.

FLORA: It's just a name, sir.

EUSEBIO: There's no such thing as "just a name." Every name means something. Even if you don't know what that meaning is and you have to spend your whole life trying to figure it out.

(Beat.)

FLORA: I don't know, sir.

EUSEBIO: And, please, it's Eusebio, not "sir." I work for a living.

FLORA: I meant no offense.

EUSEBIO: I'm not offended—God, why is this so hard?

FLORA: I'm—I don't know. Did you miss your bus again?

EUSEBIO: I just can't seem to catch that bus.

FLORA: Maybe if you left a little earlier, you wouldn't miss it so often.

EUSEBIO *(Laughs)*: Yes, you're right.

(Beat.)

FLORA: Petra's inside. I'm sure you want to talk to her.

EUSEBIO: Well, actually . . .

FLORA: Petra is probably the most beautiful girl on this island. At least one of the most outspoken—and I guess modern men like a girl who speaks her mind. Especially when she has eyes as green as hers.

EUSEBIO: Yours are green too. Like the sea.

FLORA: Oh, it depends on the light. And they're definitely not as big and wild as my cousin's.

EUSEBIO: She's not the reason I missed my bus every night for the last two weeks, Flora, and I think you know that.

37

FLORA: I'm not sure what I know, Eusebio. About anything.

EUSEBIO: May I approach?

FLORA: I don't like what people might say if they see us.

EUSEBIO: I can't stay that long. My curfew, remember?

FLORA: I ought to call Petra down.

EUSEBIO: I walked five miles to be here. I have another mile to go. And I worked a twelve-hour shift. Have mercy, please.

(Beat.)

FLORA: A minute.

(Eusebio crosses the alleyway and approaches Flora.)

EUSEBIO: I got you a beer. Rheingold.

FLORA: A beer! Oh my God, you have to be kidding! A Rheingold!

EUSEBIO: Is that no?

FLORA: Maybe girls do that in Ponce but not where I come from. Not in a million years.

EUSEBIO: More for me, then.

(Eusebio drinks.)

FLORA: How my father would kill me if he knew I was in the middle of the city, standing next to a man I don't know who's drinking a beer.

(This strikes Eusebio as funny and he laughs, drinks his beer. Looks at Flora, dying to make conversation.)

EUSEBIO: I don't really like boats, and I can't swim, so don't ask me what I'm doing in the National Guard. But when I'm on the ship, I like one thing: the feeling that this big, iron monster I'm on is floating on the water. I love how it goes so gently up and down. One night I realized that I had known that feeling all my life. This island we're on . . . this smudge of dirt in the great ocean . . . also floats, like a weightless little dream in the middle of the world, just floats along taking all its dreamers and maniacs and children with it. That's why things happen to this island yet it never changes . . . it just floats through history, happy, carefree, like nothing really matters. Sure you don't want a sip?

FLORA: I haven't changed my mind.

EUSEBIO: It would take a lot to change that mind, I see.

FLORA: Are you saying I'm stubborn?

EUSEBIO: No, no, I was just—

FLORA: Well, I am stubborn. It's not a bad thing to be. Anything goes today, like it doesn't matter, as you say, like we really do live in this floating cloud where there's no tomorrow, only the fun you can experience today. That's not my world. For me, it all matters. Every word a person says. Every thought. Why? Because we are always being watched. And I don't mean by busybodies and brujas with nothing better to do—I mean by the All Mighty Lord. And it matters to Him. But nowadays, people act likes He's blind and deaf and it's okay to say and do anything as long as it makes you feel good. That "fun" is the most important value and everything must be sacrificed on the altar of pleasure. Well, I don't feel that way, Eusebio, I think it's wrong.

(Eusebio pours the two beers onto the sidewalk.)

EUSEBIO: Okay, no fun tonight.

FLORA: You shouldn't waste beer, that's a sin!

EUSEBIO: Girl, there's no winning with you! It's all sin! Listen, I believe in God, too, but I don't really think God put us on the earth to suffer all day long. Or else we wouldn't have eyes to enjoy beauty or hips to move to music. And do other things. We'd be stones or blocks of wood. Is that a life worth living? Denying pleasure is a ridiculous way to live.

FLORA: Then I'm ridiculous. Thank you for telling me.

EUSEBIO: Might as well be dead. Or join a convent and wear a crown of thorns all day.

FLORA: If you start blaspheming, I will really have to go, sir.

EUSEBIO: Why don't you go now? Why have you spent all this time with me?

FLORA: I don't know but that's a very good question.

EUSEBIO: Because you're lonely and don't want to be alone. Because, despite your hatred of all things fun, you want to talk to me. Because you know how much fun being with a man can be.

FLORA: Yes, I'm having a ball.

EUSEBIO: You're a funny girl. Your words say one thing but your eyes tell me something different.

FLORA: First I'm stubborn, then I'm ridiculous, now I'm a hypocrite!

EUSEBIO: You know you're none of those things. You're—a fine young woman who is smart enough not to trust a man in uniform she just met on the street. A woman with a sparkle in her eyes who is carrying around something sad, a little painful, and can't trust that the world might offer her something better than the usual pain and sadness. Am I in the ballpark?

(Tears threaten Flora but the last thing she wants to do is cry in front of a stranger.)

FLORA: Everyone has sadness.

EUSEBIO: Some more than others.

FLORA *(Soft)*: Don't say any more, please? I don't want to talk about sadness, if it's okay with you.

EUSEBIO *(Soft)*: Yes, of course, Flora. I have a really big mouth.

FLORA: It's not you. You have—a good imagination and you really think about things, and I like that, even if I know you're completely wrong about everything you said. You don't let life get you down.

EUSEBIO: No, I'm not nailed to the cross like some people.

FLORA: Some people aren't as lucky as you.

EUSEBIO: Lucky? I'm the middle child of eleven. I cried myself to sleep every night of my youth. We had nothing. Just hunger and despair and the special loneliness only hunger and despair can produce. But I refused that life. I left home and worked.

I leave my job at the hospital and put on this uniform every few months. I climbed down from the cross and told it to—to kiss my—you know where I'm going with this.

FLORA: I have some idea.

(Beat. Soft.)

I'm trying to do that, too, Eusebio. And I'll be fine some day, I guess.

EUSEBIO *(Likes how she says his name)*: Are you kidding? You're going to be great.

(Flora smiles at Eusebio, liking him more and more.)

FLORA: I hope you're right.

(Beat.)

EUSEBIO: I think it's time for me to meet your parents.

FLORA: How much of that beer did you drink?

EUSEBIO: I want to see you again, Flora, but I don't want to do it on a city bench by an alleyway in the middle of Santurce. That's not how a proper girl is supposed to spend time with a man.

(Beat.)

FLORA: You want to spend time with me?

EUSEBIO: I can't think of a better way to spend my time.

FLORA: Are you married, engaged or seeing anyone currently?

EUSEBIO: That's a very strong question!

FLORA: I just don't want to waste anyone's time. Not that I'm saying I want to spend time with you, and not that I'm saying I *don't* want to spend time with you, but *if* I were thinking about spending time with you, I would immediately stop thinking about spending time with you if, you know, you were married, engaged, or seeing anyone currently.

EUSEBIO: A strong girl with strong views.

FLORA: I was a fool once and I won't do it again. I don't care if I never get married. I'd rather be alone and keep my pride than be married like a fool to a man who doesn't love me.

EUSEBIO: Isn't pride a sin?

FLORA: It's overrated as a sin. Not being smart is a bigger sin.

EUSEBIO: Can anyone really be smart about their feelings?

FLORA: Probably not.

(Thinking about this.)

Sometimes I think the heart is crazy. It doesn't know when to stop loving. I think that's the flaw God gave us to make us just a little less than the angels and better than the beasts. The flaw of loving too much or too fast or too stupidly or too blindly. The flaw of loving without reason or purpose: that's our sweet imperfection. Which is why we have to put borders around our passions and a fence around our hearts. To learn when to trust and how to express it. To learn to say "enough, I don't want to feel anymore." Or: "More, make me feel more."

EUSEBIO: I think I like the last part of that best.

FLORA: I'm saying way too much. I should go inside. Petra's going to worry.

EUSEBIO: Petra can wait. I want to know how I may meet your parents. Oh, before you say anything: I am not married, engaged or seeing anyone, as you say, currently.

FLORA: Oh, good. I mean—who cares? I haven't decided if I care or not.

EUSEBIO *(Smiles)*: Well, you take your sweet time, Flora. Look at my face and decide if you can trust me. Watch my actions and ask yourself if they're the actions of an honest man. In the meantime, I am going to Miraflores to find your family and sit down with them and we're going to talk about the weather and our families and American baseball and I'm not going to leave until I get a firm declaration from your family that it is acceptable for me to spend time with their daughter. And when

I pass that test, I am, in fact, going to spend time with you. And you are, in fact, going to take down the self-protective walls you put around your passions and dismantle the fence around your heart. And you're going to thank God for the day it was too hot for you to stay inside and a lonesome member of the National Guard missed his bus.

(Lights to black.)

Scene 6

A month later. Flora's front yard. A hot, sunny afternoon.
Don Fermín and Doña Milla on the porch.

FERMÍN: Only a month later and she wants us to meet a boy from Ponce! Everyone knows the boys in Ponce are fast and untrustworthy!

MILLA: Don't give me this nonsense about the boys from Ponce. You've lived your entire life in Puerto Rico and have never once made a trip to Ponce.

FERMÍN: It's on the other side of the earth!

MILLA: I think it's a good sign. That she can forget Manuelo so fast and start to like someone else.

FERMÍN: What are people going to think? That she's loose! It's a character flaw . . . being able to go so easy from one love to another.

MILLA: She never said she loved this Eusebio.

FERMÍN: Then why am I wasting my time meeting him?

MILLA: Oh, you have too many appointments, do you? A crowded schedule, is it?

(Flora and Petra walk to the house from the dirt road.)

FLORA: Is he here yet?

FERMÍN: Where were you?

PETRA: She was too nervous to sit and wait, so we took a walk. I love the countryside. One day I'm going to buy a house in New Hampshire, USA.

FERMÍN: What the fuck is that?

MILLA: Moncho! Your language!

FERMÍN: Every time I hear "USA" I want to curse.

FLORA: Well, don't curse when Eusebio gets here. Don't say anything controversial. He doesn't want to hear about Puerto Rico becoming independent or how we have to kill all the yanquis and how Pedro Albizu Campos was the incarnation of Jesus Christ on earth.

FERMÍN: I heard him speak in Arecibo once!

MILLA: And no one cares!

FLORA *(To Don Fermín)*: Don't drink, don't tell your voodoo stories, don't insult the National Guard, don't show him your fighting birds, and don't pick a fight with Mami about Efraín.

FERMÍN: Why don't I take some poison and die? Is this the pope coming to the house? Since when is a man censored in his own house?

PETRA: When someone's in love and she's crazy to make a good impression.

FLORA: I'm not in love. I want to make a good impression on a young man who—

FERMÍN *(Seeing someone coming up the street)*: I can't fucking believe it.

(Manuelo comes up the road to the house. He's dressed in a somber gray suit and holds a Bible.)

45

MANUELO: A good afternoon, everyone. God be with you all on this beautiful day.

(All look at him in silence.)

FLORA: Manuelo . . . we're expecting a visitor from Ponce today. He's a young man I met in Santurce last month after you—after we—broke our engagement. And this is not a good time for you to visit.

FERMÍN: In fact, asshole, it's never a good time. Milla, where's my machete?

MILLA: There's not going to be any machetes today.

FERMÍN: This man dragged my daughter's name into the gutter and mocked her virtues. I will hang his nuts from the living room wall!

PETRA: Just think of all the flies that will attract.

MANUELO: So the rumors are true, Flora. While I was in New York, you found someone else. I guess that means . . .

MILLA: . . . that she never really loved you very much? I guess that's what it means.

FLORA: It doesn't mean that at all. I did love you, Manuelo. But you killed the part of me that loved you. As for this young man I met in Santurce—

MANUELO: I have not even looked at another woman since that day, Flora, even though, in New York, they were throwing themselves at me. Your words changed everything. I stopped the idiot, selfish, childish actions of a man who only *thought* he was being a man. I didn't value you, Flora. But I'm back now, humble and naked, to tell you old Manuelo is dead. You killed him and good riddance. Let that corpse rot in the tender grave of your memories. If it was possible for Christ to rise again, why can't it be possible for a simple man like me to simply change?

FERMÍN: You compare yourself to the Lord!? That's all I need to hear!

(Don Fermín disappears into the house.
Doña Milla runs after him.)

MILLA: Moncho, what are you doing?!

PETRA *(To Manuelo)*: You have some nerve, after what you did to my cousin.

FLORA: Petra, it's okay—

PETRA: But his words mean nothing. And I know you. You'll listen and believe him—because you believe everyone's good.

FLORA: Everyone is good.

MANUELO: That's right, my angel!

PETRA: Well, just remember the snake didn't hold a gun to Eve's head—he used *words*. Sweet, musical, honeyed words that any magician with a black heart can spin and spin until you're too dizzy to think.

MILLA *(Off)*: Jesus Christ, man! You're going to drive me to an early grave!

(Don Fermín appears at the door, brandishing a machete.)

FERMÍN: Family is sacred! You must be willing to kill for it!

*(Don Fermín goes for Manuelo, machete raised.
Flora, Petra and Doña Milla try to hold him back.)*

FLORA *(Screams, overlapping)*: Papi! No!

PETRA *(Screams, overlapping)*: Do it when no one's looking!

MILLA *(To Manuelo, overlapping)*: Run, you fool!

(Manuelo throws his Bible to the ground and pulls out a tiny pocket knife.)

MANUELO: If I must fight for the hand of the woman I love, then I will fight!

FERMÍN: Bring it on, cocksucker! I'll slice you good, fuckface!

(As Don Fermín struggles against the screaming women and Manuelo gets into a fighting crouch, knife in hand, Eusebio, in civilian clothes and holding a suitcase and a beer, walks to the house from the dirt road.)

No one notices him for a moment as he watches the mayhem, amused.

Then Flora realizes he's there and nearly screams from embarrassment.)

FLORA: *Eusebio!!*

(Don Fermín stops struggling.
The women unhand him.
Manuelo pockets his knife.
All look at Eusebio, who doesn't seem perturbed in any way.)

EUSEBIO: Flora, it's a very lovely house.

FLORA *(Flustered)*: Thank you. We like it.

EUSEBIO: Hello, everyone. Hello, Petra.

PETRA: Captain!

EUSEBIO *(To Doña Milla)*: You must be Flora's mother.

MILLA: Yes. Hello. We're not always fighting.

EUSEBIO: You should meet my family. We are always fighting.

FLORA: This is my father.

EUSEBIO: My name is Eusebio Calderón and it's a great honor to meet you, sir. That's a hell of a machete you have there.

FERMÍN *(Sizing him up)*: Sharp enough to cut through anything. Including lies, hypocrisy and bullshit.

EUSEBIO: I hope you'll lend it to me some day. *(Regarding Manuelo)* And who's this?

FLORA: This is my—

MANUELO: I am Flora's fiancé, Manuelo Ramón Delgado, at your service.

FLORA: He's not my fiancé. He *was* my fiancé. But I returned his ring and ended it, as I told you.

EUSEBIO: I heard all about you, Manuelo.

MANUELO: And I know nothing of you. Our little Flora keeps her secrets very well, doesn't she?

FLORA: There's no place for you here, Manuelo. You and I had our chance, and I wasn't good enough to keep you, so it's ended.

MANUELO *(To Flora)*: Honey, if I could just talk to you *alone* for a few minutes. After two years, I deserve that much, don't I?

EUSEBIO *(To Flora)*: I think he's right. A man you've loved, even if it's in the past, has rights. And he obviously still loves you. So you two should talk. And I should get out of the way and go back to Ponce.

FLORA: Eusebio, you're not going to leave, are you? This isn't how this is supposed to happen.

EUSEBIO: The only way I can stay is for me to have a right to stay. The only way I can have that right is to be your fiancé. The only way to be your fiancé is for you to answer yes to the question, "Flora will you marry me?" So, how about it? Flora, will you marry me?

(All are silent, shocked, looking at Flora who is fighting tears of joy.

As lights go to black, Flora, Eusebio, Don Fermín and Doña Milla go into the house.

Manuelo is left alone onstage . . . he exits slowly, sadly, knowing he's lost Flora forever.)

Scene 7

A year later. Flora's front yard. Sunset is deep red and slow.

The set is dressed with Christmas lights, flowers and Puerto Rican flags—festive for a wedding party.

Lively music, talking, laughing and dancing can be heard from the house.

Doña Milla enters from the house, wearing her best dress. She walks to the garden, looking sadly at the flowers, preoccupied and distant.

After a moment, Flora and Eusebio enter from the house, flush from dancing.

Flora is in a simple white wedding dress. Eusebio wears a sharp black suit.

EUSEBIO *(To Doña Milla)*: There you are! Doña Milla—Mother!
MILLA: May the Lord bless you, Son.

(Eusebio and Doña Milla embrace. Doña Milla cries.)

EUSEBIO: Darling, what's the matter?

MILLA: On the day my daughter is married . . . Efraín is so far away. He doesn't even know what's happened. Maybe he'll never know.

FLORA: God will bring him back, Mami.

MILLA: He's forgotten us. He's someone else now. That's what happens to people who go up there.

(Flora and Eusebio look uncomfortably at each other.)

FLORA *(To Eusebio)*: We have to tell them, Pito . . .

EUSEBIO: As soon as we can, Mita.

(Petra and Don Fermín enter, in their best clothes.)

FERMÍN: This is what I live to see. This old house full of people and dancing. Food and children!

PETRA: Soon there are going to be a lot of those running around this house, eh Flora?

FLORA: Well, there's something Eusebio and I need to . . .

EUSEBIO: Gather round, everyone! I'll make an announcement to my family and the others in a minute. But I want to tell you first what Flora and I have decided to do.

FERMÍN: You don't need to do any more, you've already made us very happy.

FLORA *(Torn, upset)*: You and Mami gave us a beautiful day.

EUSEBIO: A day we'll always remember. But even a beautiful day like this is one small step in a long journey.

(Beat.)

As everyone knows, the island, our island, which we love so much, is in pain. As beautiful as it is, for many it's an island of tears. Men like me are losing their jobs. Good people go hungry.

MILLA: What's he saying, Flora?

FLORA *(Trying not to cry)*: I'm so sorry, Mami . . .

EUSEBIO: Well, I think men and women must make their own destiny. Not blindly accept the destiny that's given to them. And I won't sit by and do nothing as my new family goes hungry.

FERMÍN: What's he talking about? Flora?

EUSEBIO: That's why Flora and I have made the painful, but necessary, decision to—to leave the land we love so much and move to the United States . . .

FERMÍN: Is he kidding me?

EUSEBIO: . . . to find work, make money, live a decent, prosperous life and give our children a real education . . .

FERMÍN: You're taking my daughter—up *there*? To that *slum*? To the drug addicts and prostitutes? And snow?

FLORA: Papi, it's something we both decided—

MILLA: No. Not my girl. Not my only girl.

EUSEBIO: She's my girl now, Doña Milla.

MILLA *(To Flora)*: You promised me.

FLORA: I've been thinking about this and Eusebio is right, Mami. There's no future here for a young—

FERMÍN *(To Eusebio)*: From the moment I met you, I thought you were a gringo-loving, arrogant snob!

FLORA *(To Doña Milla)*: We'll visit as much as we can—

MILLA: You'll have children I'll never know! They'll speak *English*!

FLORA: Mami, you always told me a woman's duty is to follow her husband—

MILLA: Not to America!

FERMÍN *(To Flora)*: And you have to be here when your brother comes home.

EUSEBIO: Don Fermín, your son is never coming home.

(Doña Milla runs into the house.)

PETRA *(To Flora)*: I can't believe you're going there before I am!

(Going into the house.)

Milla! Doña Milla!

(Petra is in the house.)

FERMÍN *(To Flora and Eusebio)*: I've seen it before. Good people flee the material poverty of the island. Only to find the spiritual poverty up north is worse than anything they ever imagined. If you take her, Eusebio, I will curse you. Your life will be nothing up there. Nothing.

(Don Fermín disappears into the house.
Eusebio and Flora are alone in the garden. They look at each other. Eusebio is determined to go no matter what.
Flora wavers, torn by her conflicting loyalties.)

EUSEBIO *(Holding out his hand)*: Flora?

(Flora thinks . . . then takes Eusebio's hand, sealing her decision and her fate. Lights to black.)

Act Two

·)|(·

SCENE 1

Thirty-eight years later, spring 1992.

Daleville, Alabama, a small town adjacent to the Fort Rucker Army Base.

Flora and Eusebio's house is nicer than Flora's childhood home in Puerto Rico, yet small and poor by North American standards. Cheap linoleum floors, thin walls, everything seems vaguely toxic.

The living room has secondhand furniture. A door to the outside world. On the walls are a colorized portrait of Don Fermín and Doña Milla, photos of Flora and Eusebio in their youth, their many children and a photo of a young, smiling Petra.

There are many potted plants and flowers—as if Flora were trying to re-create her mother's little garden in Puerto Rico.

Flora, now sixty-one, played by the actress who played Doña Milla, is in the living room, watering plants.

Flora is strong, sharp, and in good health. Flora has subtly but undoubtedly been North-Americanized.

In the bedroom are a small cot and a large hospital bed. A folded wheelchair in the corner.

Eusebio, now sixty-six and played by the actor who played Don Fermín, lies on the hospital bed.

Eusebio's legs have been amputated from the knees down. He's had a minor stroke which has limited the use of his left hand. Above his bed is a chin-up bar.

A small TV on a dresser at the foot of the bed faces Eusebio. A sitcom quietly plays. There's a coffee maker next to the bed.

Like Flora, he has been subtly North-Americanized over the years.

Eusebio searches his bed for the TV remote and can't find it. Calls out:

EUSEBIO: Flora!

(Flora talks to the plants as her mother used to.)

FLORA: You! As my mother would say: I'm not even talking to you! Don't give me that look!

EUSEBIO *(Desperately)*: Flora! *Flo-raaaa!!*

(Flora hurriedly puts the watering can down and goes into the bedroom.)

FLORA: What's the matter?

EUSEBIO: The remote.

FLORA: Jesus Christ, I thought you were dying.

EUSEBIO: The Mets!

FLORA: You're going to die if you don't watch the Mets?

EUSEBIO: It's the home opener!

FLORA: You're being ridiculous.

EUSEBIO: The Mets make me happy.

FLORA: I thought you said they suck.

EUSEBIO: They do suck, but they make me happy.

FLORA: Baseball has never made sense to me.

(Finds the remote.)

Here it is.

(She turns off the TV.)

EUSEBIO: What are you doing? Turn it back on!

FLORA: There's something I have to tell you.

EUSEBIO: If you make me miss the opening pitch . . .

FLORA: What? You're going to get up from that bed and chase me around the house? Listen to me. This is important.

EUSEBIO: I never thought you'd be capable of so much cruelty.

FLORA: You don't know what cruelty is, Eusebio.

EUSEBIO: You want to switch places with me? I think I know something about cruelty, Flora.

FLORA *(Instantly repentant)*: Pito, I know, I know, I didn't mean . . .

(Flora leans over and kisses Eusebio. They hold each other—and Eusebio deftly takes the remote from Flora.)

EUSEBIO: Ha! Victory belongs to Eusebio Calderón!

(Eusebio goes to aim the remote at the TV, but Flora stands in the way.)

FLORA: Something is going to happen today that you have to know about.

EUSEBIO *(Frustrated he can't see TV)*: ¡Me cago en na'!

FLORA: *Listen.* I'm losing my mind with boredom. I want to do something to help out the church. We had a meeting last night.

EUSEBIO: Kept me up half the night with your stupid tambourines.

FLORA: Passion is not stupid, Pito. Now, you know everyone's worried about all the kids in the church getting married too young. At sixteen and seventeen they think they know what marriage is. Well, last night the church decided that someone very smart, with a lot of experience with marriage, should counsel kids and help them—

EUSEBIO: You volunteered for this, didn't you?

FLORA: Yes, because it's important.

EUSEBIO: Fine. Now spread your legs or get out of the way.

FLORA: This affects you, too. I'm going to bring in young people to spend time with us. That's *us*. To watch how you and I get through the day as a married couple.

EUSEBIO: Why would anyone want to do that?

FLORA: So they can see what marriage really is. So they don't rush into it and ruin their lives.

EUSEBIO: Oh God, what a terrible idea. These kids will take one look at us—a religious fanatic and an old drunk with no legs—and run for the hills.

FLORA: Well, it's done.

EUSEBIO: But you're giving me no choice, Mita. How fair is that?

FLORA: You think I've had choices in my life? You think a Puerto Rican woman of my generation had real choices?

EUSEBIO: Oh, God, no—not a history lesson!

FLORA: Is it a sin to be useful? You think being your nurse is all I want in life?

EUSEBIO: Yes, bring these kids in! Let's show them what a happy marriage is really like!

(A knock at the front door.)

FLORA: It's them—the first couple.

EUSEBIO: Today? Now?

FLORA: They're getting married in a week.

(More knocking.
Flora takes the remote from Eusebio.)

EUSEBIO: If the Mets lose because I'm not watching them, it's completely your fault, woman.

(Flora quickly combs Eusebio's hair, making him more presentable.)

FLORA: Sexy man!

(Flora crosses to the front door of the living room and opens it. Standing there are Monica and Oskar.
Monica is twenty-three, shy, dark-haired, played by the actress who played Petra in Act One.
Oskar is her fiancé, twenty-seven, a private in the U.S. Army, played by the actor who played Eusebio in Act One. Monica and Oskar are very nervous.)

Hello? Monica and Oskar?
MONICA: Yes, Mrs. Calderón. How are you?
FLORA: Please call me Flora and welcome, come in.
OSKAR: Thank you, ma'am—Mrs. Flora.

(Monica and Oskar come in. Stand in the living room awkwardly.)

Would you like something to drink?
MONICA: No thank you, we're okay.
OSKAR: Only if you've got some whiskey.
FLORA: Oh no, we don't have anything like that!
MONICA: Oskar's kidding.
OSKAR: Not necessarily.
FLORA: We never have any alcohol in the house . . . not since my husband got sick.
So—how long have you been in the church?
MONICA: I was raised in the church. Oskar is new. I got him involved after we got involved.
FLORA *(To Oskar)*: How do you like it?
OSKAR: Oh, it's a barrel of laughs.
MONICA: I think he finds some of the rules a little too much.
OSKAR: And I thought the army was bad!

MONICA *(Quick)*: Well, I think it's great that you're doing this Doña Flora.

OSKAR: Have you done this before?

FLORA: No, you're my first ones.

OSKAR: You're not a professional?

MONICA: Oskar, Christ—

FLORA: I have thirty-eight years experience, Oskar. I've slept with no other man but Eusebio. If that doesn't make me qualified to discuss marriage, then I don't what does. Now, how long have you two known each other?

MONICA: Two months.

FLORA: Two months and you want to get married?

OSKAR: See? All they want to do is judge!

FLORA: Where did you meet?

MONICA: In Daleville. In a bar. He picked me up.

OSKAR: You make it sound so sleazy.

MONICA: True love is never sleazy!

FLORA: The important thing is that you love each other. Do you love each other?

MONICA: Oh God, very much.

OSKAR: The fact that I'm here, putting up with this, *proves* I love her.

FLORA: Good. Love has to be there. Some young people get married because someone needs a green card, or, well, the girl is, you know, pregnant?

MONICA: Oh, that's not us.

OSKAR: Definitely not us.

MONICA: Not us in a million years.

OSKAR: Im-possible.

FLORA: In my day, a girl was a virgin on her wedding night. It was terrifying. And thrilling. And confusing. And happy. And something happened in that bed that was profound and beautiful and . . . well, these days girls don't have that experience. They jump in the sack first chance they get. And they miss the biggest night of their lives.

MONICA: No, we haven't done it yet.

OSKAR: Not us in a million years!

MONICA: Im-possible!

FLORA: But that was an old time that disappeared with so many other sweet things. *This* world: too fast for me! I couldn't be young now.

MONICA: Doña Flora, I know two months seems like nothing . . . but I'm so sure. Oskar's the one. Everything I ever wanted in a man. In one nice, yummy, eye-pleasing package.

OSKAR: Isn't she friggin' great? Hottie!

MONICA: You're the hottie!

(Oskar and Monica kiss, furtive, hungry.)

FLORA: Well, okay, if there's nothing else, I guess we should start. Eusebio is right through here.

(Flora motions them to follow her into the bedroom.
Eusebio looks up at Oskar and Monica as they enter.
The sight of the legless Eusebio has an immediate sobering effect on the young couple. It seems to have a greater impact on Monica than on Oskar.)

Eusebio Calderón, my husband.

OSKAR *(Offering his hand)*: Hello, sir, Private First Class, Oskar Garcia.

EUSEBIO *(Shaking his hand)*: Private Garcia, welcome. Did she tell you I was in the National Guard?

OSKAR *(Salutes Eusebio)*: No—but that's great, sir.

EUSEBIO: And who's *this* . . . ?

MONICA: Monica Santoro, sir.

EUSEBIO: It's very good to meet you, young lady.

(Eusebio smiles, reaches out his hand. Monica offers her hand and Eusebio kisses it.)

MONICA *(Charmed and a little nervous)*: Not many men kiss your hand anymore.

FLORA: Yes, my husband is a real, old-fashioned gentleman.

(Extremely awkward silence.)

Well, as you can see, my husband is having some health problems that have affected the whole family—

EUSEBIO *(To Oskar)*: Can you believe she's doing this during a Mets game?

OSKAR: Who're they playing?

EUSEBIO: Braves.

(Eusebio and Oskar do the Braves' "tomahawk chop" and laugh together, bonding.
Monica smiles nervously, not sure what to make of all this.
Eusebio smiles, points at Monica.)

I saw that pretty smile! And such eyes! Glorious!

FLORA: That's enough, Pito. We know you appreciate female beauty.

EUSEBIO: In my time we made a woman feel like she's a *woman*. Even if she was the ugliest thing on two legs and had a mustache—if she was your woman, no one was more beautiful. And you told her every single day of your life.

MONICA: Did you hear that Oskar?

OSKAR: I'm learning a lot from this man already.

FLORA: Yes, my husband is a treasure trove of wisdom.

EUSEBIO *(Expansive)*: Marriage! People think you lose yourself in marriage. No, you *find* yourself. Young lady, why don't you sit next to me?

MONICA: I don't know if it's safe getting too close to you, Don Eusebio.

EUSEBIO: You got that right.

OSKAR *(To Eusebio)*: Too much, man! I want to be just like you!

(Flora clears her throat, ready for the business at hand.)

FLORA: The first thing you'll notice is that there are two beds in the room. I sleep on the little cot. Eusebio and I haven't slept together in the six months since his operation.

OSKAR *(Whisper, to Eusebio)*: Can you still, you know . . . ?

EUSEBIO *(Making "fucking" gesture)*: Can I still . . . ?

MONICA: Oskar, what a question!

EUSEBIO: Baby, at my age, that's the only question worth asking!

FLORA: Pito, for the love of God in Heaven—

EUSEBIO *(To Oskar)*: Do I look like a man who's been getting some?

FLORA *(Determined to do this)*: When I wake up, I open the blinds and let the sun in. The sunshine is good for his skin. Then I start the coffee.

(Eusebio grabs the chin-up bar and pulls himself up with his good hand.)

EUSEBIO: But I can still do pull-ups!

OSKAR *(Laughs, to Monica)*: We'll have to get one of those for our bed!

EUSEBIO: My marriage advice? Do it as often as you can, as long as you can, everywhere you can.

FLORA: I keep the coffee maker by his bed because he likes the smell and it reminds him of Puerto Rico.

EUSEBIO: She likes to ignore me when I talk about sex. But don't let her fool you. The more religious they are, the hotter they are, the more they want it and the rougher they like it.

OSKAR: Right on, brother!

(Oskar and Eusebio high-five.
Monica laughs.
Annoyed, Flora does a little show-and-tell.)

FLORA: I keep all his medications here. Emergency phone numbers. Insurance papers. I turn him over so he doesn't get sores. Help him in and out of his wheelchair. I find the baseball games on TV and *Jeopardy*. And of course, the Bible. The word of God is the greatest medicine.

EUSEBIO *(Sotto to Oskar)*: Debatable.

(Oskar stifles a laugh.)

MONICA: God, there's so much to remember; I don't know if I . . .

EUSEBIO: Hey, young lady! I wasn't always like this. Mita, tell them I wasn't always like this.

FLORA: He wasn't always like this.

EUSEBIO: Tell them how amazing I was.

FLORA: He was—

EUSEBIO: Coño, I had legs when we first met. I came to America with hope. Remember, Mita? The strength I had?

FLORA: Of course I do, Pito, but sometimes it hurts to remember . . .

EUSEBIO (*On a roll*): No one worked harder. There wasn't a job I wouldn't do. No matter how bad it paid or how degrading.

FLORA: They weren't hiring Puerto Ricans for anything good back then.

OSKAR: They're still not, Doña Flora!

EUSEBIO: I did everything. I was a cook in a greasy spoon in Lake Ronkonkoma. Making ninety bucks a week—for five years.

FLORA: Every year he went to his boss Mike, begging for a raise.

EUSEBIO: Ten more bucks a week was all I wanted. Mike always said no.

(*An alarm goes off.*
Flora checks the medicine schedule and administers Euse-bio's medicine during the following.)

FLORA: And Pito, this proud man, kept flipping burgers in silence, because he had a family to support.

EUSEBIO (*Taking the medicine*): Until I told Mike to stick his job up his ass. Then I was a janitor in my kids' high school . . . Christ . . . one time I went in the boys' locker room to clean up some vomit and the whole football team was waiting for me. As soon as I walked in, the little monsters pelted me with toilet paper, jock straps and tampons.

OSKAR: Christ is right.

(*Flora takes Eusebio's temperature. Records it on a chart.*)

EUSEBIO: Then I tried what all good Americans try: my own business. A little broken-down diner in Comac with a jukebox that screamed that ugly American rock everyone loved so much. Then they opened a mall across the street serving cheap fast food. And Flora got cancer. And I—couldn't go on anymore—I lost the business and almost lost my wife. I almost lost my Flora.

(Tears threaten Eusebio and he stops.)

MONICA: Maybe this isn't a good day for us to be here . . .

(Not wanting to succumb to tears, Flora starts clipping Eusebio's fingernails.)

FLORA: Thank God it wasn't my time to go. I was needed here.
EUSEBIO: I don't know what I would have done if God had called you . . .
FLORA *(Fighting tears)*: Okay, okay, okay—now we're depressing these poor kids, Pito!
EUSEBIO *(To Oskar and Monica)*: I'm sorry kids, I didn't mean—
OSKAR *(Wiping his eyes)*: It's okay, sir . . .
MONICA *(Wiping her eyes)*: We should probably go soon.
FLORA: I get so caught up in taking care of him, I forget there was any other life but the one right here.
EUSEBIO: You do! You forget all the good times we had!

(Flora reaches over and takes a photo of their old house and shows it to Oskar and Monica.)

FLORA *(Tries to smile)*: We had such a pretty house. Sure, it was a little broken down but we liked it. Long Island was still so green back then—I even liked the snow at first! Like the sky was playing a crazy game with us. We danced in it like children the first time. We made nine kids in that snow.

MONICA: Christ, nine.

EUSEBIO *(Quiet)*: Three of them died very young.

FLORA *(Her mind far away)*: I'm not sure, but I think something of those winters rubbed off on the souls of our children—something a little dark, pessimistic, lonely . . . something so foreign to the easy sunshine of the people we knew in Puerto Rico.

(Silence a moment as Flora wipes her eyes.)

EUSEBIO: Still, we managed to send two of them to college. The others joined the military. We traveled the U.S., living near our children . . . ending up here when our son Pablo was stationed in Fort Rucker.

OSKAR: Really? Maybe I know him.

FLORA: He was sent to Germany. Just last week.

EUSEBIO: Now we're stuck, alone, in this red-neck town, except for those tambourine-waving hags from the church and none of them can sing worth shit.

FLORA: The loneliness has been the hardest part.

EUSEBIO: Yes. It's worse than not walking.

(In the silence, Flora hands Eusebio the remote.)

FLORA: We can leave you alone now, Pito.

(Eusebio takes the remote. Looks at the TV. At the young couple.)

EUSEBIO: Sometimes I think her father Don Fermín went to the local witch and put a spell on me the day of our wedding.
    (Regarding his missing legs) It started with one toe. I stubbed it one night . . . but there was so little feeling in it, I didn't know anything was wrong. Until I noticed the dead-meat color and the smell and knew that not all of me was alive. They cut it off. Then, another toe. Half the foot. The other foot. Doctors, saws, anesthesia and waking up with less and less. I got shorter each month.

(Beat.)

All my life, before I became a stump, I struggled against God's fate and thought fatalism was the Puerto Rican's poor excuse for never taking action, or rising up in anger to demand independence or justice or power. But the joke was on me. God's fate was a lot stronger than I knew. He planted me in this bed like a flower in dirt and now I can't get out, no matter how much I dream of running, running, running.

(Silence as all take this in.)

FLORA *(Indicating the TV)*: It must be the third inning by now, Pito.
EUSEBIO: I got lucky, though, I married a woman with sea-green eyes and endless energy. Nine children couldn't exhaust her.

(Beat.)

This woman, this industrious, indestructible woman stays with me, bathes me and wipes my shit every day without a break. And all I have to do is put up with the sound of tambourines! If you can't imagine yourself doing this for someone else, if you can't get your hands dirty, if you can't stand the smell or the pity or the pain in the other person's face, if you'd rather be anywhere else, then you're not ready to be married, my young friends. Call it off. Because it's this or it's nothing.

(Short silence as Oskar and Monica take this in.)

MONICA *(To Flora)*: And you don't want to run away?
FLORA: Every day. I cry, I get mad, I blame him, I blame myself. I beg God for a different life . . . but, in the end, I don't walk away.
EUSEBIO: And I, actually, can't. But sometimes I lie on this bed . . . and it gives me that feeling I used to get in Puerto Rico . . . that sweet, dreamy, floating, moonlight feeling I always loved . . . oh-oh! Nature calling!

FLORA *(To Oskar and Monica):* Do you mind waiting in the living room?

OSKAR: Roger that.

(Oskar and Monica go to the living room to wait.
In the bedroom, lights to black as Flora helps Eusebio with the bed pan.
Monica can't look at Oskar.)

MONICA: Oskar, honey, I don't know.

OSKAR: You don't know what?

MONICA: This. Getting married. I don't think I can do it, Oskar. Fuck, I actually said it! I'm so sorry!

OSKAR: Girl, what are you talking about?

MONICA: I can't be like Doña Flora. I'm not a saint! I'm way too selfish to get married!

OSKAR *(Almost laughs):* You're not selfish. *Scared* maybe . . .

MONICA: I know me. I'm not industrious or indestructible. And let's face it, you could never do all that for me and that's okay.

(Oskar looks at Monica and thinks carefully before speaking.)

OSKAR: But I would. Exactly like Doña Flora, twenty-four/seven, no questions asked.

(Beat.)

MONICA: But how can you know? How can anybody know?

OSKAR: For the mother of my children? I'd do fifty times more than that.

MONICA: If I was in a bed with no legs and we never do it anymore and I look like death and smell like old crap and my tits hang down to my ankles and my hair looks like a vulture's nest? You'd stay with that Oskar?

OSKAR: Hmmmm, your tits hang how low?

MONICA: I knew it!

OSKAR *(Smiles)*: For real, Monica, that's the dumbest thing you ever
asked in your life . . .

*(Oskar takes Monica in his arms. The young couple hold each
other, scared and strangely exhilarated.*

*Flora comes into the living room from the bedroom—and
just watches them. Lights to black.)*

Scene 2

Eight months later. Night.

    There's a Christmas tree in the living room.
    Flora sleeps on the cot, Eusebio in the hospital bed.
    Eusebio's having a bad dream. He tosses and turns. Groans.
    The sound wakes Flora. She sits up to look at him.

FLORA: Pito, what's the matter?

(Flora gets out of bed, turns on the light, goes to Eusebio and shakes him, wakes him up.)

EUSEBIO: God!
FLORA: Pito, you're having a bad dream.
EUSEBIO: Oh my God, Mita, oh my God.
FLORA: I'm right here.
EUSEBIO: Ay—Flora—I've been *contacted.*
FLORA: Do you want some water?

EUSEBIO: By an angel! I was contacted by an angel of God tonight!

FLORA: Yes, you were full of dreams tonight.

EUSEBIO: But this was *real*. She talked to me. She was in this room. You were sleeping. She said: "Eusebio, you're going to die soon."

FLORA: That's stupid.

EUSEBIO: You're supposed to be the religious one of the family and you say a message from the beyond is stupid?

FLORA: It wasn't a message, it was a nightmare, now go back to—

EUSEBIO: I saw her better than I see you. And she told me what you and all the doctors won't: that I'm about to die. That God has decided to take me and all this waiting around is a waste of time.

(Angry, Flora leaves the bed, goes to the light.)

FLORA: Why do you want to upset me like this? Talking about death like it was your favorite baseball team!

EUSEBIO: I didn't ask the angel to visit me!

FLORA: There was no angel! You're being morbid and doing that thing I hate: feeling sorry for yourself.

EUSEBIO: But I don't. Can't you see how happy I am? She said my suffering is about to end.

FLORA: God help me, he's losing his mind too.

EUSEBIO: I don't have to be a prisoner anymore. I can walk and be strong again. And when you come to Heaven, we'll make love there!

FLORA: Yes, *years* from now.

EUSEBIO: No, this week. The angel said I croak two days before Christmas.

FLORA: Sick! A sick imagination, Pito!

EUSEBIO: We must prepare.

FLORA: Yes, first we get the straitjacket, then we get the little men in the white coats . . .

EUSEBIO *(Imitating an angel)*: "Solemn preparations must be made for the imminent death of Eusebio Antonio Calderón." Then she said something in Latin. In *Latin*, Mita!

FLORA: Ridiculous!

EUSEBIO: In the morning you're going to call the funeral home, and the children. You and the kids can pick out a coffin. Not too expensive, but nice. Wood not metal. I'm a man of the earth, remember, the soil and water are part of me even if the years in America have cut me from my roots. I want to be buried in Miraflores. Make sure the flowers are wild and full of color. Don't be cheap with the flowers.

FLORA: For Godsakes, shut up Eusebio! You're fine. Your blood pressure is down. Your blood sugar is stable. You're getting more movement in your fingers—

EUSEBIO: I die of a heart attack this Friday night.

FLORA: Aggh! Why do you torture me like this?

EUSEBIO: But it'll be in my sleep and I'll never feel it and then there's peace—for you, too! You won't have to kill yourself taking care of me.

FLORA: I like to take care of you, idiot. That's what I'm supposed to do.

EUSEBIO: No, it's not. No one deserves this. You have no life outside this room except the old brujas and their church songs. Prisoner to my body. That's you. I want you to be free.

FLORA: Some day, yes. When God wills it. But He hasn't willed it yet. It was a dream only, my love. Forget it and go back to sleep.

EUSEBIO: And last rites, Mita. I demand last rites.

(Flora, exhausted, just looks at him, trying to figure a way out of this.)

FLORA: Okay. If you promise not to talk about this anymore, I'll get you a priest and he can perform your stupid last rites. I don't care.

EUSEBIO: It has to be before Friday.

FLORA: It will be before Friday because on Saturday you're going to wake up and realize what a fool you've been and you're going to apologize for putting me through so much crap. And I'm going to laugh my ass off.

(Lights to black.)

Scene 3

Two days later.

Eve, twenty-five, a young Spanish nurse played by the actress who played young Flora, checks Eusebio's blood pressure and his bed sores, and records her findings on Eusebio's chart.

EUSEBIO: What time's he coming?

FLORA *(Off)*: A couple of minutes, Pito.

EUSEBIO: Are you coming to my funeral, Eve?

EVE: There's not going to be any funeral, Don Eusebio. Everything inside there is doing just fine. Long as you take the medication, do your pull-ups, stay clean and dry, keep the positive attitude, you're gonna live longer than me.

(Flora enters with a clean shirt for Eusebio.)

FLORA: I say nothing.

EUSEBIO *(To Flora)*: What did the funeral home say?

FLORA: They can't actually schedule a wake until there's been a *death certificate* which doesn't happen until there's an actual *death*. Crazy gringo laws, I don't know.

EUSEBIO: I guess you can take care of all that Saturday morning.

EVE: I'm rubbing cream here, 'cause that psoriasis is acting up. And, look, Monday, I'm giving you a haircut. You're getting a little bushy up there.

EUSEBIO: There will be no more haircuts or Mondays for Eusebio Calderón.

(This sounds so pompous, Flora tries not to laugh.)

EVE: For a guy who's about to face the big one you're pretty cheerful.

EUSEBIO: Who wouldn't be happy, the angels waiting for you with a new pair of legs, all your ancestors in a Heaven that looks like Puerto Rico in the 1890s, when we were liberated from Spain. And you can drink all the beers you want with Jesus and it doesn't mean shit.

FLORA: Don't say those blasphemous things, Pito, please.

(Eve and Flora help Eusebio into the shirt. Flora combs his hair as Eve gathers her things.)

EVE: I know you don't believe me, Don Eusebio, but I'll see you next week, okay?

EUSEBIO: Time. Not my problem anymore, Eve.

(Eve and Flora exchange glances. Flora walks Eve out of the bedroom and into the living room.)

EVE: How long's he been like this?

FLORA: Should I worry?

EVE: We can look into psychological services.

FLORA: Oh, he'd never do that.

EVE: I think he's still depressed from the surgeries. A year is not a long time to get over the loss of your legs.

FLORA: Sometimes he just starts crying. I play music from our youth—an old bolero, like he used to love so much—instant tears. I mention one of the children, or they call on the phone, or I show them a picture of the grandkids. He can't stop himself.

EVE: At least the idea of dying makes him smile.

FLORA: Look, maybe you should stay when the priest comes. I don't know what he's going to be like and I might need some help with him.

(Beat.)

EVE: He reminds me of my father so much.

FLORA: Was he crazy, too?

EVE: Hard to say. There was nothing mysterious about him except everything about him was a mystery. He died before I ever got to ask him so many things. What do you really *want*, Dad? What do you dream about, Dad? Do you believe in anything except the next paycheck, Dad? How can we thank you for ruining your life for us, Dad?

(Beat.)

Men like that . . . one day, the weight of all that work and sadness breaks their backs and they collapse. When my father finally stopped moving long enough for me to catch up with him and hold him . . . he was so old and sick, he had no words left . . . he lost the habit of talking and we never had a real conversation. He built our house, he fed me, he loved my mother, he created my brothers and sisters, and I didn't know who he was.

(There's a knock at the door.)

Of course I'll stay.

(Flora goes to the door, opens it.

A Priest is there, played by the actor who played young Manuelo.)

FLORA: Father, welcome.

PRIEST: Flora, my dear.

FLORA: This is Eve de la Rosa, Eusebio's nurse.

EVE: Hello, Father, how are you?

PRIEST: A little confused.

FLORA: Not half as confused as I am, Father. He thinks he's dying, no matter what I or Eve or the doctors say.

PRIEST: So we're just humoring him.

FLORA: I just want to get through this week and go back to normal. But I don't want to waste your time either.

PRIEST: Eusebio is scared. He doesn't want to be surprised by death. He wants to be smarter than death.

(Beat.)

FLORA: Do you think he's dying? That there was an angel?

EVE: Flora, there's no way—

FLORA: In his soul? His heart's been broken too many times—and he just wants to stop?

PRIEST: The only two who can know are Eusebio and his Maker.

EVE: Flora. A man who flirts as outrageously as Eusebio, believe me, ain't ready to be dead.

FLORA: This isn't life . . . this unhappy lump in that bed . . . this insult . . . this betrayal . . .

PRIEST: He loves you, Flora. That keeps him alive, if nothing else. Love is the last thing that goes.

FLORA *(Deep breath)*: Okay. Saturday morning I'm going to be so mad at him for putting me through this—this—

EVE: This *shit*. Say it. It's shit, Flora.

PRIEST *(Laughs)*: Thank you for putting it in perspective, Eve. Let's go in.

*(Flora hesitates a moment, then leads the Priest and Eve into
the bedroom.*
  Eusebio looks up at them, all smiles.
  Flora tries not to betray her anger and discomfort.)

EUSEBIO: Father. It's great to see you, sir.

PRIEST: Good to see you, too. How are you doing today?

EUSEBIO: Dying, sir.

PRIEST: So I hear. You look pretty sharp for a man about to leave
the material world behind.

EUSEBIO: Soon I'll be looking sharp and dancing my bottom off in
Paradise, sir.

PRIEST: I guess if you have to die, you might as well do it with a
positive attitude and a smile on your face.

EUSEBIO: You only die once, sir!

FLORA: This isn't funny, Eusebio! This isn't a joke!

EVE: Flora, it's okay, honey, please . . .

FLORA: If this is true, and you're really going to leave me alone and
make me face life without you . . . how can you be so damn
smug?

PRIEST *(To Eusebio)*: You see how much pain this is causing? You
know no one on earth wants you to die, Eusebio, and God
doesn't think death is a joke. He put us here to test our souls
and there's no escaping these trials except through death—the
only mechanism that tears the wall between flesh and spirit.
The trouble is, Eusebio, every cell in your body is designed
by nature to resist that exit and the violence needed—the
necessary *apocalypse* it takes to destroy that will to live—is
the most terrible ordeal a man or woman can ever face. You
understand, Eusebio?

EUSEBIO: Yes.

PRIEST: Are you sensitive to the fact that death's worst victims are
the ones that are left behind to grieve and regret?

EUSEBIO: Yes.

PRIEST: Look at Flora now. Look at her good. See the way time has
changed her. The effects of a long life on her skin, hair, her eyes,

the shape of her torso, her heart. See the ways you've written on her body, Eusebio: how your actions have curved her skin, as if everything you've done to her has been accompanied by a signature you etched in her flesh. "I was angry at you today, Flora," signed Eusebio. "I was thoughtless today," signed Eusebio. "I did not do my best for you today," signed Eusebio. These autographs mar the perfect skin of the young lover she was and now you see her as she is: wrinkled by time and by you.

(Beat.)

Now look at Flora and remember that night in Santurce, thirty-nine years ago. Remember the sky. The hot streets. The sway of the bolero you played on the jukebox to get her attention and how you intentionally missed the bus every night for two weeks so you could walk by her window. And how she watched you from that window, every night! Remember the overpowering attraction. The mystery you wanted to solve: "What is it like to kiss you, Flora? What is it like to feel your naked skin on mine? What is it like to enter you?"

EVE *(A little shocked)*: Father!

PRIEST: Yes, I am graphic because I must be graphic! Because love isn't meant to be veiled or prettified or perfumed. It's about *union*. Merging two in one. The opposite of the sin in the Garden of Eden, when one unity became two and opposites were born in the world. God seeks union with us—but that can't be obtained in life. It can only happen after death. And the physical, emotional union we feel with a lover is only the overture, the tender hors d'oeuvres of union with God. Eusebio, when you first saw Flora, you wondered what union with her would be like: that was the mystery she offered that only she could solve—and she did: many, many, many times. Right?

EUSEBIO: Uh-huh.

PRIEST: So please know this is serious, this is not a game, Flora's heart is not your playground. I'm not going through with this unless you're dead serious about being dead.

EUSEBIO *(Barely audible)*: Serious, sir.

PRIEST: Okay. Fine. Let's do this. The first step in dispensing last rites to the dying is confession, which I can't give if there are others present.

EUSEBIO: They can stay, I don't care.

PRIEST: It's your funeral.

(The Priest crosses himself.
   Eusebio, Flora and Eve cross themselves.)

Eusebio Antonio Calderón, are you ready to confess in order to cleanse your soul and make it worthy to be in the presence of the Infinite?

EUSEBIO: I am.

PRIEST: Speak.

EUSEBIO: I was arrogant and thought my body was indestructible because it had never failed me. So I didn't listen to the doctor who told me I had diabetes and I continued to smoke and drink beer. I gambled money I should have used on groceries and clothes. I fought over stupid, little things that meant nothing. I cursed God when they cut my legs. I struck my children. I did a thousand other things, Father, big and small . . . but the worst thing I did . . . I didn't love my Flora enough . . . not the way she should have been loved . . .

FLORA: No one could have loved me better.

EUSEBIO: But I strayed. I, I couldn't stay faithful to my wife, Father. As hard as I tried, and God knows I tried, I couldn't do it.

FLORA: Angel, that's old, old news. I've forgotten what happened between you and Soledad Esparza, you know this. I know you're sorry and there's no need—

EUSEBIO: I don't mean Soledad Esparza.

(Beat.)

FLORA: What do you mean you don't mean Soledad Esparza?

79

(Beat.)

EUSEBIO: I don't mean Soledad Esparza when I say that I strayed from you.

FLORA: You mean there was someone *else*? Before Soledad Esparza?

EUSEBIO: After. She was after.

FLORA: You mean, after your affair with Soledad Esparza—and all the hell that unleashed—you had an affair with yet *another woman*, Eusebio?

EUSEBIO: I'm— *(To the Priest)* I'm dying, right?

PRIEST: Don't look at me, I'm not a doctor!

EUSEBIO: This is a confession on my dying bed, Flora, I must confess everything.

FLORA: You had an affair with another woman after I forgave you for your affair with that ugly cunt Soledad Esparza!?

EUSEBIO *(To Priest)*: Is she supposed to be talking during last rites?

FLORA *(To the others)*: I can't believe him! Can you believe him? I know I can't!

PRIEST: I do find myself at a major loss for words.

EUSEBIO *(To Priest)*: I think you need to tell those two to leave so we can continue, Father.

FLORA: Oh, we're going to continue, my love. I want to hear all about this. *(To the Priest and Eve)* You two can go now.

EUSEBIO: What are you doing? How can I confess without a priest?

FLORA: You have a higher authority to answer to than God and that's me, pal.

PRIEST *(To Flora)*: Are you sure?

EVE *(To Flora)*: Is it safe to leave you two alone?

FLORA: Good question. Sorry I can't answer it.

EUSEBIO *(To Priest)*: You can't let her interfere with the wishes of a dying man!

PRIEST: You're upset, Flora. I understand. But he is a helpless, sick man who can't defend himself right now—

FLORA: Fine! I don't care! *(To Eusebio)* It's all yours, my dear. Let's hear your confession. We and God are ready to hear every name, date, and detail. You will leave nothing out. Not one moment of fucking.

EVE: Oh my God.

FLORA: Yeah, oh my God. The man is dying, after all, let's hear his final story. I bet it's a good one.

(Silence.
    All look at Eusebio, who is very uncomfortable.)

EUSEBIO: Well, shit, maybe that angel was just a dream . . .

(Lights to black.)

Scene 4

Saturday morning. The sun barely starting to rise.

Flora asleep on her cot. Eusebio in the hospital bed, asleep, very still and quiet.

Flora awakens. Sits up, rubs her eyes, gets her bearings. Looks over at Eusebio, who isn't moving at all. Scared, she approaches him.

He doesn't seem to be breathing.

Flora touches him.

FLORA: Pito? It's Saturday.

(No response from Eusebio.

Flora shakes him hard. Still no response. Flora tries to keep from panicking.)

Pito—wake up!

(She practically hits him and Eusebio wakes with a start. He quickly looks around—at the dingy, little bedroom, the unhappy walls . . . the stern-looking wife at his side.)

EUSEBIO: Mita?

FLORA: Guess what, big boy.

EUSEBIO: Where am I?

FLORA: Where are you? In Daleville, Alabama, my love. In our sad excuse for a bedroom, still without your legs but still very much alive.

EUSEBIO: This is a mistake.

FLORA: It sure is, and you made it.

EUSEBIO: It's still Friday!

FLORA: Saturday morning. Past your expiration date.

EUSEBIO: The angel made a mistake!

FLORA: Dreams don't make mistakes, dream *interpreters* do.

EUSEBIO: Are you sure this isn't Heaven?

(This makes Flora laugh out loud, possibly the funniest thing she's heard in years.)

FLORA: Heaven! Oh my God, I can't wait to tell the girls at church! Eusebio says this shithole is Heaven! Oh God, I'm gonna pee-pee!

EUSEBIO: Something has gone wrong, Flora.

FLORA *(Laughing)*: Yes, it sure has. Unbelievably wrong.

EUSEBIO: Stop laughing.

FLORA: I knew about the first one. Even before you told me. I could *smell* it. And after I got over the shock . . . the anger, the grief, the *second* round of anger and the hysteria that followed *that* . . . then the first, actual, painful forgiveness and coming closer as I tried, like a tiger, to hold this thing we created, this family, together . . . after all that, you put me through this *again?* . . .

EUSEBIO: You can't forgive a little weakness? . . .

FLORA: A few days ago, you broke my heart, Eusebio, in a way I didn't think was possible anymore. I really thought the part of my heart that feels jealousy was dead . . . but you brought it back to life. And made me feel pain older than the world.

EUSEBIO: Flora, for the love of God, it was twenty years ago.

FLORA: Not the secrecy—which lasted until this week. All this time you knew . . . and you let me go on, ignorantly happy, pretending you had changed, not knowing the truth about you and where your mind was, what your memories were—your simple, stupid wife working her ass off, the house-slave who didn't deserve the truth until it was almost too late. And if you dare tell me God made men and women different, I will vomit!

EUSEBIO *(Trying not to cry)*: Why did the angel do this to me?

FLORA: You better hope your angel hasn't fallen asleep, because you're going to need all the supernatural protection you can get.

EUSEBIO: I'm not supposed to be here anymore, Flora, I'm not . . .

FLORA: Well you are. And you might as well face the fact that I am furious with you and, guess what? You can't walk to the nearest bar and give yourself a little amnesia.

EUSEBIO: Don't make me feel worse than I feel.

FLORA: Don't tell me what to do. You don't decide what I do. I trusted you and believed in you and this is what you give back? Well maybe you can call your old girlfriend—get her to come down here and clean your shit for you.

EUSEBIO: Oh God . . .

FLORA: You know I still get letters from Manuelo? Telling me he still loves me? And how he'd divorce his third wife for me? He's a big deal in television, he's a rich man, and what are you? You're *nothing* . . .

EUSEBIO: Will you stop that?! Will you stop beating me?! Will you stop insulting me?! I can't get up! I can't walk away! I am trapped and you continue to lash me without mercy! For what? A stupid, twenty-year-old infidelity! Stop it!

(Eusebio's outburst silences Flora for a moment.)

FLORA: You owe me.

EUSEBIO: Then take what I have. Take my money! Wait—there isn't any! Take my freedom! No, that's gone too! Take my ability to fuck, take my love of God, take my shoes, take my curiosity, take my laughter, take my hope—no, wait, you can't, can you? Because all that's been flushed away, taken by the doctors and trash collectors, the rats and worms and—

(Eusebio stops. His eyes go big.
Something happens in his mind, as if an invisible hand were inside it, an irrational presence erasing everything it touches.
He shakes his head, turns his head to the side as the stroke slices him.
Silence.
Flora looks at him and can see the unmistakable change in his lusterless eyes.)

FLORA: Pito? Pito, what happened?

(Eusebio looks up at her and can't respond. His power of speech is gone.)

Pito! Talk to me! Pito, say something to me!

(Eusebio's attempt at speech is a long slur of sound.)

Oh my God. Oh my God in Heaven. Oh Holy God!

(Flora goes to the telephone and dials.)

Eve! Come over right now! Come over—please! It's Pito!!

(Lights to black.)

Scene 5

Two months later. Night.

The Christmas tree is gone.

In the bedroom is a big Valentine's Day balloon and flowers.

As Eusebio sleeps, Flora watches over him, stroking his fore-head, quietly saying a prayer over him.

A knock at the front door. Surprised, Flora leaves the bedroom, goes to the living room door and opens it.

Oskar and Monica are there. Monica holds their newborn baby in her arms.

FLORA: Oskar! Monica! What a nice surprise.

(Oskar and Monica enter. They exchange hugs and kisses with Flora.)

OSKAR: We have someone we want you to meet. Born on Valentine's Day.

(Monica holds out the baby, who Flora takes in her arms.)

FLORA: Oh, she's so beautiful.

MONICA: That's Oskar's face totally, right?

OSKAR: We hope that changes as she gets older.

FLORA *(To the baby)*: May God bless you and keep you, angel-angel!

MONICA: She's a pretty good sleeper too.

FLORA *(To Monica)*: How do you feel?

MONICA: Like I could have eight more, actually!

OSKAR: Christ! Thank God those days are over.

FLORA: Ay! These days women have two babies and they think they've *done* something. Two is a warm-up! Are you hungry?

OSKAR: No, no, thanks, we can't stay too long.

FLORA: I'm so glad you came. Marriage suits you both. I knew it would.

MONICA: How's Eusebio, Flora?

FLORA: He's okay.

OSKAR: You know, I still can't believe what happened to him.

(Beat.)

FLORA: Yes. I miss his conversation.

OSKAR: He was so damn funny.

(Oskar does the "tomahawk chop.")

MONICA *(The baby)*: We'll have to teach it to Isabelle.

FLORA: I know he can understand everything. And the doctor says he might learn some words again and, in a few years, if God wills it, he'll be flirting and making jokes.

MONICA: What about you?

FLORA: I'm fine.

(Beat.)

OSKAR: Do you think Eusebio could see the baby? Would he even know it's us?

(Beat.)

FLORA: He should sleep. He doesn't sleep enough.
MONICA *(Hands her photographs)*: You can show him these.

(Beat.)

FLORA: What time is your flight?
OSKAR: Typical army nonsense, we leave at oh-five-hundred, the ass-crack of dawn.
MONICA: We're going to write and call you every single day.
FLORA: That gets a little expensive all the way from Germany!
MONICA: No, we're not going to lose touch. You're our family now, Doña Flora. We owe you one marriage and one baby.
OSKAR: With eight more to come, according to her.

(Beat.)

FLORA: Maybe you'll find Pablo out there.
OSKAR: I'm definitely going to track him down, Doña Flora.

(An awkward silence as they all realize its time for the young couple to go.)

MONICA: Well, we should get going. We've got a lot of packing tonight.

(Flora kisses the baby.)

FLORA *(To the baby)*: Good-bye. I don't know when I'm going to see you again, my Isabelle.

(Flora hands the baby to Monica.)

MONICA: Doña Flora, I'm going to miss you!

(Monica and Flora embrace and kiss.)

OSKAR: Me, too. Good-bye!

(Oskar and Flora embrace and kiss.)

FLORA: Have a safe journey and God will watch over you. I know he will.

(Oskar and Monica leave.
  Flora closes the front door. Locks it. Stands at the door of the silent house and tries not to cry but is overcome . . .
  Lights to black.)

Scene 6

Two months later. Night.
> *The Valentine's Day balloon and flowers are gone.*
> *Eusebio on his hospital bed watches the Mets on TV.*
> *Flora stands behind him, giving him a shave.*

FLORA *(Regarding the game)*: Who's winning?

(Eusebio struggles to say "Mets" and it comes out:)

EUSEBIO: Mhhytshh.
FLORA: Go Mets. What is it? Two-nothing! Wow! Good way to start the season, Pito. This could be the one!
EUSEBIO *("Yes")*: Yyshhh.
FLORA: Are those bums going to find a way to blow this one too?
EUSEBIO: Yyshhh!
FLORA *(Laughs)*: Well, have faith, maybe they hold on to the lead this time.

(The other team suddenly gets three runs on a homer off the Mets' starter.)

EUSEBIO *("Shit")*: Shhhyt!
FLORA: No!
EUSEBIO: Shhyt! Shhhyt!
FLORA: They blew it again! I can't believe this!
EUSEBIO: Shhhtypyd Mhhyshhh!
FLORA: Stupid Mets is right. You want me to turn it off?
EUSEBIO: Nnoh!
FLORA: I'll never understand the pleasure you get from this, Pito.

(Flora finishes the shave and looks at him, pleased with her work.)

You want to see?
EUSEBIO: Yyshhhhh.

(Flora holds up a mirror so Eusebio can see the shave. He smiles as best he can.)

FLORA: Good, huh? What a handsome man!
EUSEBIO *("Yes, handsome")*: Yyshhhh. Hundshhymm.

(Eusebio, unable to stand the sight of himself, looks away.
Flora gets up and blocks Eusebio's view of the game on the TV.)

FLORA: I have to talk to you about something important.
EUSEBIO: Mhhyshhh!
FLORA: Look, you already know the ending, they're going to lose.

(Flora turns the TV off.
Eusebio sulks.)

EUSEBIO: Byytshhh.

FLORA: Did you just call me a bitch?

EUSEBIO: Yyshhh.

FLORA *(Laughs)*: Asshole!

(She playfully slaps him but it's clear she's more amused by his comment than angry.)

I've been talking to Eve. You know how much she loves you. The both of us. Before she went back to Spain, she got me these.

(Flora reaches into a pocket, pulls out a bottle of pills.)

Remember the angel who came to you in your sleep? Eve figured out a way to grant the angel's promise. With these.

(Beat.)

I'll take them, too, Pito. We'll go together. You understand? No more bed. No more pain. And maybe in Heaven, the Mets win the World Series every year. I know you've been wanting to do this for a long time and I resisted it because I thought it was a sin to wish for your own death. To play God with yourself. But now I'm so confused and I want you to not suffer anymore, my angel—no more! And if God can forgive me, maybe we'll be all right.

(Beat.)

You want to?

(Eusebio thinks about this a moment, stares at the pills in her hand.)

EUSEBIO: Nnohh.

FLORA: No? Are you sure?

EUSEBIO *("I'm sure")*: Ahhh shuursh.

FLORA: You want to stay here? Like this? Are you sure, Pito?

EUSEBIO: Yyshh.

FLORA: Why?

EUSEBIO *(Struggles, "With you")*: Wysshh ewyu.

FLORA: With me?

EUSEBIO *("With you, Flora")*: Wyshhh ewyu, Foohah.

FLORA: Okay. That's okay. With you, Pito, with you.

> *(Flora wipes her eyes.*
>
> *She throws the bottles of pills into the trash. Picks up the remote and turns on the Mets game.*
>
> *Eusebio holds out his bad hand. He struggles to open it . . . and he does.*
>
> *Flora takes his hand and gets into bed with him.*
>
> *In the distance Flora and Eusebio, young, holding hands, and dressed as they did in 1953, appear. They look at their older selves.*
>
> *As the sound of the game gets louder and louder, lights go to black.)*

END OF PLAY

Brainpeople

·)⁜(·

Special thanks to Erica Gould, Rebecca Wisocky, Mozhan Marno, Jessica Boucher, Jennifer Blevins, Robert Clyde, Avery Clyde, the Mark Taper Forum Mentor Playwrights, Lisa Peterson, Marissa Chibas, Svetlana Efremova, Jessica Hecht, Jacqueline Kim, Ana Ortiz, Michi Barrall, Juliette Carrillo, Sandra Oh, Morgan Jenness, Len Berkman, Jerry Patch, the Black Dahlia Theatre, Scott Horstein, Nick Mangano, the Garson Theater, Madeline Brown, Lindsey Marlin, Desi Moreno-Penson, Zenda Tatoyan, Hartford Stage, Playwrights Horizons, Tim Sanford, Jeremy B. Cohen, Lisa Timmel, the Public Theater, Johanna Pfaelzer, Karina Arroyave, Zabrina Guevara, Camillia Monet, Alyssa Bresnahan, Primary Stages, David Lee Strasberg, Carlos San Miguel, Juan Carlos Malpeli, Benoit Beauchamp, Sidney Miller, Vahe Berberian, Lyon Forrest Hill, Jennifer Mae Stevens, Kárin Tatoyan, Javi Mulero, Lina Patel, Ariane N. Picari, Vaishnavi Sharma, Dana Eskelson, Sherri Barber.

Production History

Brainpeople was commissioned by South Coast Repertory (David Emmes and Martin Benson, Artistic Directors; Paula Tomei, Managing Director). *Brainpeople* was made possible by the generous support of the William and Flora Hewlett Foundation for New Works, an endowment fund of the Next Generation Campaign.

On February 2, 2008 *Brainpeople* received its world premiere at the American Conservatory Theater in San Francisco (Carey Perloff, Artistic Director; Heather M. Kitchen, Executive Director). It was directed by Chay Yew. Daniel Ostling was the set designer. Lydia Tanji was the costume designer. Paul Whitaker was the lighting designer. Cliff Caruthers was the sound designer. June Palladino was the stage manager. The cast was as follows:

MAYANNAH	Lucia Brawley
ROSEMARY	René Augesen
ANI	Sona Tatoyan

Characters

MAYANNAH, an aristocratic Latina, mid-thirties
ROSEMARY, white, working-class, late thirties
ANI, Armenian, a designer, early thirties

Setting

Mayannah's apartment, Los Angeles.

Time

The present.

Note

There is no intermission.

When you sleep in the exile's bed linen or drink from his cup do you know his body or his name?

—*THREE APPLES FELL FROM HEAVEN*,
MICHELINE AHARONIAN MARCOM

I felt a Cleaving in my Mind—
As if my Brain has split—
I tried to match it—Seam by Seam—
But could not make them fit.

The thought behind I strove to join
Unto the thought before—
But sequence raveled out of Sound
Like Balls—upon a Floor.

—EMILY DICKINSON, 1864

A tiger comes to mind. The twilight here
Exalts the vast and busy Library
And seems to set the bookshelves back in gloom;
Innocent, ruthless, bloodstained, sleek,
It wanders through its forest and its day
Printing a track along the muddy banks
Of sluggish streams whose names it does not know
(In its world there are no names or past
Or time to come, only the vivid now)
And makes its way across wild distances
Sniffing the braided labyrinth of smells
And in the wind picking the smell of dawn
And tantalizing scent of grazing deer;
Among the bamboo's slanting stripes I glimpse
The tiger's stripes and sense the bony frame
Under the splendid, quivering cover of skin.
Curving oceans and the planet's wastes keep us
Apart in vain; from here in a house far off
In South America I dream of you,
Track you, O tiger of the Ganges' banks.

—"THE OTHER TIGER" BY JORGE LUIS BORGES,
TRANSLATED BY NORMAN THOMAS DI GIOVANNI

Light reveals a long, empty table covered in a colorful tablecloth decorated with images of the Taino Indians of Puerto Rico.

  Lights comes up to further reveal Rosemary/Rosie. She is in her late thirties; slight, working-class, pretty, but hungry and worn down by life. Her clothes, shoes and costume jewelry were bought at the Salvation Army. Her overdone makeup is a little trashy. She speaks in an Irish accent to an offstage person.

ROSEMARY/ROSIE: God, I haven't had meat in so long. I forgot how much I loved the *smell*!

  (Expanding light reveals a once-luxurious penthouse apartment in downtown Los Angeles.

  Seen through big windows, a red sun sets, forcing the sky into strange, startling colors.

  As time passes, sparkling city lights appear—until the view outside feels like an urban dreamscape, as removed from crime, fear, distress as possible.

*There's exposed brick; a once-fancy fireplace with miss-
ing tiles; distressed wooden floor; faded furniture; old books;
morbid artwork; folkloric, graphic crucifixes; naked statues of
Jesus. Everything was once brightly colored, vibrant, but is
now muted and decayed—as if the room were stuck in time.*

*Mayannah enters from the kitchen holding a fancy but-
ter dish. She is mid-thirties, with long dark hair, dark, intense
eyes; her clothes are elegant and black; she wears diamond
necklaces, earrings and bracelets. Her sad, lovely, aristocratic
Puerto Rican face is heart-shaped.)*

MAYANNAH: This butter was made from the milk of cows born and
raised in my parents' hometown in Puerto Rico.
ROSEMARY/ROSIE: Red meat, blood and butter! Wow!
MAYANNAH: Every year I get it flown from the island on a private
jet just for this meal.
ROSEMARY/ROSIE: I love that pretty necklace. So glittery.
MAYANNAH: My mother left it for me.
ROSEMARY/ROSIE: And it's absolutely incredible, this *place*, Mayannah.

(Mayannah pours rum.)

MAYANNAH: Comes with the best Puerto Rican rum in the world.
My family's own label!
ROSEMARY/ROSIE: Like a big, bloody church. All the pretty Jesuses!
MAYANNAH: I collect them. From all over the world.
ROSEMARY/ROSIE: Why are they all naked?

(The doorbell rings.)

MAYANNAH: Ay! That must be her! The other one! I thought she'd
never show!

*(Mayannah goes offstage. The sound of a door opening.
Rosemary/Rosie hungrily stares at the butter on the table.)*

ANI *(Off)*: Hello Mayannah? It's, it's Ani. I'm here. In one piece thank God!

MAYANNAH *(Off)*: Yes! So glad you're here, Ani!

(Rosemary/Rosie sticks her finger in the butter and tastes it.)

ROSEMARY/ROSIE: Oh good God, *that's bloody fucking fab . . .*

(Rosemary/Rosie hungrily drinks the butter and licks the dish.)

ANI *(Off)*: Your home—so dark—but beautiful!

MAYANNAH *(Off)*: You are beautiful! I had no idea!

(Mayannah leads Ani, early thirties, into the room.
Ani is a brilliant, beautiful, obsessive, lovelorn Armenian woman with porcelain skin, piercing eyes beneath glasses. Hair in a ponytail.
Though articulate and well-dressed there's something awkward about her: she has a hard time navigating real and emotional space.)

ANI: Yeah, well, last time you saw me, I looked like death.

(Mayannah leads Ani to Rosemary/Rosie.)

Oh, someone's already here. Hi.

MAYANNAH: Ani—please meet Rosemary.

ROSEMARY/ROSIE: God, don't call me that awful name. That bitch! That loser! She was not fucking bloody invited! It's Rosie.

MAYANNAH: Oh, I meant—Rosie . . .

ANI: Hello. Nice to meet you, Rosie.

ROSEMARY/ROSIE: Yeah, okay.

ANI *(To Mayannah)*: I brought some wine. I don't actually know anything about wine but I read in a pretty good wine magazine that this is a pretty good bottle of wine.

MAYANNAH: Thank you so much, that's so thoughtful.

(Ani hands Mayannah the wine.)

ROSEMARY/ROSIE *(Under her breath)*: Wine mag? Lame!

ANI: So they—they put up these new checkpoints on the 10 . . .
God, those soldiers are the dumbest, most Neolithic men in
America! They asked for my ID and it took forever. Lucky
that your driver had all that cash. Or else I never would have
gotten here.

MAYANNAH: Well, you're here with friends now and everything's
going to be magic.

ANI: Magic? Is that a good thing? . . .

(Mayannah looks admiringly at her two guests.)

MAYANNAH: Oh, you two: lovely eyes, lovely hands . . . and we're all
really here—in my house—the three of us.

ROSEMARY/ROSIE: Three! Oh, brother!

MAYANNAH: So this is the part where I officially thank you guys for
braving the crazy streets and coming all the way here to be
with me tonight.

ANI: Well, thanks for having us.

ROSEMARY/ROSIE: That goes double for me! Triple, even!

MAYANNAH: The rule is, whatever happens on the street tonight, it
doesn't touch us. Up here we will have as much fun and be as
happy as we can.

ANI *(Trying to kid)*: Oh—no pressure!

MAYANNAH: I have a feeling . . . you two are going to be the best
guests I ever had.

ANI: So all we have to do is . . . *eat*, right?

MAYANNAH: And talk, *really* talk—no holding back, either of you—I
didn't go through all this trouble to talk about the weather!
At the end of dinner . . . there'll be a little monetary reward
for you two, as we already discussed . . . then everyone goes
home . . . easy, right?

ANI: Cash, check, or wire transfer?

ROSEMARY/ROSIE: Not to put the cart before the horse, but would it
be kosher to get my hundred G's in crisp, new five-dollar bills?

MAYANNAH: Make it to the end of dessert and you might get the keys to the whole, damn house!

ROSEMARY/ROSIE: Awesome!

MAYANNAH: Okay, now—there's a lot to do. And I do it all myself. That's my rule.

ANI: Why wouldn't we make it to the end of dessert?

(Mayannah goes off to the kitchen.
Ani and Rosemary/Rosie regard each other awkwardly.)

So . . . you don't know her either?

ROSEMARY/ROSIE: First time for me.

ANI: *First* time?

ROSEMARY/ROSIE: Technically, the second time, I guess. But it's the first time for me.

ANI *(Letting that go)*: She seems nice . . . a little—uhm, *odd*—bit gloomy . . .

(Mayannah appears with platters of tostones, which she puts on the table.)

So! I, I changed outfits like eighteen times. It's been forever since I got asked out. Didn't know people still did that. Have dinner parties.

MAYANNAH: Because people are too afraid.

(Rosemary/Rosie is drawn to the food like the starving person she is.)

ROSEMARY/ROSIE: Well, sure, all the curfews and tanks and—*that looks yummy.*

MAYANNAH: People were afraid before the curfews. Let's face it, people *terrify.* La Doña always tells me: nothing on earth can scare you like another human being.

(Mayannah goes off to the kitchen.)

ANI: Thought I was the only one who thinks depressing shit like that.

ROSEMARY/ROSIE: You must think you're pretty special, then.

ANI: No, it's just—people worry me. You can't trust what they do or say. Like everyone around here is speaking their own language. And nobody tells the truth!

(Mayannah enters with a steaming platter of rice and beans. She puts it on the table.

She puts out serving spoons, long knives, cleavers, long forks, skewers and corkscrews.)

MAYANNAH: Absolutely true!

ANI: Isn't that how we are? Always hiding from each other—so we never know what's really going on?

ROSEMARY/ROSIE: When do we stop the yakking and start the eating?

ANI: It's like we're geniuses at keeping the really good stuff—the far-too-easy-to-break stuff—buried so deep, no one can touch it. It makes me feel like I have to be a damn archaeologist half the time, always digging below the surface of people, hoping, you know, for *answers*, some *clarity*, an actual, real glimpse at a person's, you know—*soul*.

MAYANNAH: An archaeologist of personalities!

ANI: Yes! It's like a defense thing with me. So I don't get tricked or smashed or fucked, the way I look at people.

MAYANNAH: I noticed that about you. You keep staring at me and, uh, Rosie—

ROSEMARY/ROSIE: I'm sorry, but it gives me the heebies, all your staring, all your eyeballs googling at me.

ANI: I don't think of it as staring. I think of it as *analyzing*, like an X-ray.

ROSEMARY/ROSIE: "Annie," is it?

ANI: Ahni . . .

ROSEMARY/ROSIE: Let me just say, Auuhhni, that maybe you shouldn't dig too deep. Could hurt somebody.

MAYANNAH: Or scare yourself to death.

ANI: Good! It's called self-examination?

ROSEMARY/ROSIE: Well, I don't want anyone exploring me. Cracking my head open to look inside.

MAYANNAH: You won't look her in the eye. I noticed that about you.

ROSEMARY/ROSIE: Or listen to the words in my head. Some nights it's like the bloody BBC in there! Okay?!

ANI: Hey, back off a little!

MAYANNAH: There's some tension between you two and that's not what I'm paying for—

ANI: All I'm saying, okay, someone tells you to choose between being Socrates unsatisfied, or a pig satisfied. Obvious answer: Socrates.

ROSEMARY/ROSIE: Because pigs end up like this. On a *plate*.

MAYANNAH: It's not pig. In fact, it's not even remotely *piglike*.

(Mayannah goes off to the kitchen.)

ANI: Excuse me? What's she serving us?

ROSEMARY/ROSIE *(Shouting to Mayannah)*: So, Mayannah, how rich are you, anyway?

ANI: Look, if she's serving us people . . . *not staying.*

MAYANNAH *(Off)*: A lot fucking rich.

ROSEMARY/ROSIE *(Shouting to Mayannah)*: You never count it?

MAYANNAH *(Off)*: I don't like to think about the money.

ROSEMARY/ROSIE: If it was mine? I wouldn't think of anything else. It would be the air in my lungs and the man in my bed. And I would use it to get the hell out of this country but fast.

ANI: Amen to that.

MAYANNAH *(Off)*: Sometimes I think I should be living on the street . . . wallowing in filth . . . but my poor parents would not have wanted that for me . . .

ROSEMARY/ROSIE *(Shouting to Mayannah)*: Are they dead?

(Mayannah reenters, holding a huge steaming platter of meat covered in bright red juices: organs, glands, legs, claws, muscles— bloody. She sets it on the table.)

MAYANNAH: Dead as the meat on our table.

(Ani and Rosemary/Rosie look at the unusual viscera on the table. It doesn't look like any meat they've ever had.)

ANI: Okay, you're going to think I'm—tell me it's not a *person*, okay?
MAYANNAH: You're too cute, Ani! A person!
ROSEMARY/ROSIE: I've never smelled anything like it. It has a hypnotic kinda scent.

(Mayannah takes in the table full of sumptuous food.)

MAYANNAH: Well, this is it, girls, tonight's meal.

(She is pleased, relieved this night has finally come.)

My parents bought these plates the first week they were married. The tostones and the arroz con gandules are the way we made them for generations. And the meat . . . very special. Special for tonight. For my two special guests.

(Mayannah pours three shots of rum, hands out the shots and raises her glass.)

¡Salud, dinero, y amor!

(Ani and Rosemary/Rosie raise their glasses with less enthusiasm.)

ANI AND ROSEMARY/ROSIE *(Ditto)*: Genatzet. Cheers.

(The rum takes Ani and Rosemary/Rosie's breaths away, but has little effect on Mayannah, who drinks continuously.
Mayannah lights long black candles. She puts napkins, glasses of water, loaves of bread and other finishing touches on the table, then carefully watches Ani and Rosemary/Rosie interact.)

MAYANNAH: So Ani, mi amor—didn't you just bring Socrates into the conversation?

ANI: Well, I don't know if what I said makes any sense—the self-examination thing?

ROSEMARY/ROSIE *(A little competitive)*: Well, sure, you try to live up to these socially imposed, impossible-to-live-up-to standards of beauty . . .

MAYANNAH: Wealth. Sex.

ROSEMARY/ROSIE: . . . sex, status, boob size—it's enough to make you barking mad if you think about it too much.

ANI: Still, it's better than being naive and satisfied with your unexamined self—leaving your heart open—getting your central nervous system chain-sawed by a man you thought actually *loved* you. Who actually gave two shits about you. But turns out all he wanted to do was fuck with your head!

MAYANNAH: Has someone had her heart broken?

ANI: It's just—I look around and it's like everyone's lost their souls. Did someone come and steal our souls when we were sleeping?

ROSEMARY/ROSIE: She didn't answer your question, Mayannah. Dodgy, that.

ANI: On the street, in bars, at home, every person out there . . . soulless, unreal. Like we're dead or dying or fake or faltering. Who could connect like that? Who could love like that? You want a relationship with a man? You might as well shadowbox with ghosts. You might as well make love to the wind.

ROSEMARY/ROSIE: Grim, sad world you live in, Ani.

ANI *(Smiles, tries to joke)*: Yeah, well, I'm Armenian.

MAYANNAH: They make beautiful, provocative women in Armenia, I say.

ANI: They named me after the ancient capital of Armenia . . . Ani.

ROSEMARY/ROSIE: Never heard of it. Bet it's a dump.

ANI: That poor, old city . . . destroyed so completely, visited by death so often, forgotten and lied about so relentlessly . . . smashed into so many little pieces, it's nothing but dust and sadness now. No one lives there anymore or remembers what it used to look like . . . like it never existed.

MAYANNAH: Is that how you feel, Ani? Like you don't exist?

ANI: What were my parents trying to tell me? What was I supposed to inherit with a name like that?

ROSEMARY/ROSIE: Well, in Dublin we were busy surviving. We never obsessed about love and death like you Americans. Or you Armenians.

ANI *(Skeptical about the accent)*: Dublin? . . .

ROSEMARY/ROSIE *(Impatiently eyeing the food)*: So? What are we waiting for?

(Mayannah finishes her preparations.)

MAYANNAH: Done! Girls—we're ready. Everyone. Sit. Now.

(Mayannah sits at the table, in the center.
Rosemary/Rosie and Ani sit on either side of her. Mayannah looks at Ani and Rosemary/Rosie with great satisfaction.
Rosemary/Rosie eagerly serves herself the arroz con gandules and shovels it in her mouth. Her first solid food in days.
Ani munches on a tostone, wary and watchful.)

ROSEMARY/ROSIE: I'll be *buggered*. I didn't know rice and beans could be so bloody luscious.

MAYANNAH: Told you. Ani—better not tell me you're not hungry. That's against the rules.

ANI *(Worried about the meat)*: I'm working on it.

ROSEMARY/ROSIE: I can't believe you've done all this by yourself, Mayannah.

MAYANNAH: The whole staff got the night off. La Doña—she's the incredibly old woman who runs my life—El Doctor, El Cocinero, all of them. Every year, on this night, I make them leave me alone. I have to promise them I'll be okay with strangers.

ROSEMARY/ROSIE: Some day I'm going to have my own staff—and armed soldiers, like you, May!

ANI: If you don't have a private army, you're not safe in this country.

MAYANNAH: The soldiers were La Doña's idea. They're supposed to keep us safe in case the food riots start again. Oh my God, those riots! "Eat the rich! Eat the rich!"

ROSEMARY/ROSIE *(Quietly taking up the chant)*: Eat the rich! Eat the rich! Eat the rich!

MAYANNAH: But the soldiers don't make me feel any better . . . the way they look at me . . . the dirty things they whisper . . . "I'd like to fuck her! I'd like to fuck her!"

(Unconsciously sliding into melancholy.)

I haunt this place, I don't really live in it. I don't even see the staff much. I hear them. El Cocinero gossips about me. La Doña goes through my stuff looking for the weird drugs El Doctor gives me. I don't think that old witch is ever going to die. There's no way I'll ever be friends with these people.

(Catches herself, tries to laugh.)

¡Ay Dios! All I know is—all these people cost a fortune to feed.

ROSEMARY/ROSIE: Well, I don't think we're ever going to be happy or feel safe, period. At least I'm not. So to hell with it and pass that lovely plate of glands over there.

(Mayannah happily serves Rosemary/Rosie and Ani the exotic-looking meat.)

MAYANNAH: It's tiger. And it's amazing.

(Silence at the table. Neither Ani nor Rosemary/Rosie are sure they heard right.)

ROSEMARY/ROSIE AND ANI: Did you say "tiger"?!

MAYANNAH: Can't wait for you guys to try it!

ANI: You never told us we were going to eat . . . *tiger.*

ROSEMARY/ROSIE: We're having bloody *tiger*! Is it hard to get? Like is it U.S. Government Inspected?

MAYANNAH: El Cocinero gets it for me every year. Swears it's legal. Frankly, girls, I don't want to know.

ANI: Is it like eating a cat?

MAYANNAH: It's like nothing you ever had. It's unreal.

ROSEMARY/ROSIE: He looks beautifully unreal to me.

MAYANNAH: She. Female.

ANI: We're eating a girl tiger?

MAYANNAH: Oh, yes! Mommy tiger was shot between the eyes and died in a splendid, red turbulence of blood. She left behind a whimpering little family wandering India, trying to remember what that bitch looked like.

ANI: That is fucked on so many levels.

MAYANNAH: No, there's justice to it. Animal justice. I may never eat greens again.

(Ani pushes the meat away.)

ANI: Think I'll just work on the nice tostones for now.

ROSEMARY/ROSIE: Lightweight!

(Rosemary/Rosie hungrily spears a slab of tiger meat. Mayannah watches Rosemary/Rosie like a hawk. Rosemary/Rosie puts the meat in her mouth . . . it's almost too delicious to believe.)

Hmmm . . . Jesus, *yeahhhhh* . . .

MAYANNAH: It's inside you now!

ROSEMARY/ROSIE: I don't know if it's delicious because it's delicious, or it's delicious because it's endangered!

MAYANNAH: Filling all your cells!

ROSEMARY/ROSIE: I mean, how do you describe this taste?

MAYANNAH: I know what it tastes like. It tastes like sweet revenge.

ANI: O-kay . . . cryptic . . .

(Mayannah eats the tiger meat . . . she relishes its taste.)

MAYANNAH: Do you girls ever ask yourselves . . . every time you put meat in your mouth, is the cliché true: are we really what we eat?

ANI: I—maybe—you mean—*literally*—?

MAYANNAH: When I eat this tiger . . . will I know what she knew? Will I be able to feel her mother's tongue licking her at birth? Will I know the thrill of the chase, the delicious heat of mating, and the sunsets in India?

ANI: Is that physically possible?

ROSEMARY/ROSIE: I am so totally going to India some day!

MAYANNAH: And if a tiger ate me . . . would she taste my personality and know my experiences? Would she know my childhood stories and dreams and every book I ever read . . . would she love the same music I love . . . would she love the same people? In every cell of this tiger, imagine: there's information . . . stories of the past . . . *memories.*

ANI: Jesus.

MAYANNAH: And what happens when a tiger gives birth? Is all the knowledge in the tiger's stomach passed down, genetically, from mother to child? Generation after generation? So, in a strange way, if you're eaten by a tiger . . . do you basically live forever?

(Ani and Rosemary/Rosie are struck silent by this.

    Mayannah is sliding into a private abyss of memories and obsessions.)

It's funny. So many changes happen in your life. Babies to adolescents to old age . . . always going from one state of matter to another: like water goes from ice to steam. Especially when you die and you're buried. Flesh goes to dust, blood goes to soil, mind goes to air.

(Beat.)

But—if you're cremated? Does everything in your flesh and in your mind just float off with the smoke and ash? It makes you wonder, doesn't it: what's in the air right now?

ROSEMARY/ROSIE: Or *who* is.

MAYANNAH: Yes! Who!

ANI: Thanks for contributing that!

MAYANNAH: Whose life did you just suck into your lungs? How many times a day do you take in the evaporated dreams and remains of other people? And when you breathe in that smoke, carrying all that information and life—does it change you?

ROSEMARY/ROSIE: Could explain mood swings.

ANI: What? No! Mood swings are caused by chemical reactions in the brain. I read that in a pretty good science mag—

MAYANNAH: My parents were cremated. I think of their final fire a lot . . . their fingers burning . . . eyes melting into their heads . . . their memories of me turning to smoke . . . their life stories floating in the air . . . oh, how I wish I could've breathed them in! I wish I had a chance to feel their ashes and odors filling my lungs . . . God, just one last contact with the young lovers who conceived me . . . that would've been so sweet . . .

(Mayannah's reveries are interrupted by police and emergency sirens screaming far below.

Hundreds of them seem to be streaming by, sending waves of fear and foreboding through the women.)

No! Not tonight, Dios, por favor!

(Rosemary/Rosie cringes in her seat.)

ROSEMARY/ROSIE: *No, no, no . . .*

(Mayannah and Ani go to the window.)

MAYANNAH: Thank God, they're not coming here . . .

ANI: I saw one of their sweeps in my neighborhood and it's sick how they grab people up and herd them in their vans.

MAYANNAH: There's never been a sweep down here . . . it must be something else . . . they're looking for someone.

ANI: Better not be one of you guys.

MAYANNAH: We can't worry about them tonight, Ani—I still have my soldiers. Let's sit down and eat. You haven't touched your tiger.

(*Mayannah leads Ani back to the table.*
Rosemary/Rosie is frozen in her seat, muttering . . .)

ROSEMARY/ROSIE: . . . *no, no, no* . . .
MAYANNAH: Rosie?
ROSEMARY/ROSIE: . . . *no, no, no* . . .

(*In mid-sentence Rosemary/Rosie changes personalities, becoming Rosemary/Rosalind.*
When Rosemary changes personalities, everything about her can alter: her race, accent, IQ, body language, gender and emotional makeup.
Rosalind is forties, aristocratic, arrogant, a slight mean streak in her.)

ROSEMARY/ROSALIND: —No, no, no, I'm sorry—but I'm starting to find this conversation a little horrendous. Count on Rosemary to get invited to the worst party in the city.

(*Ani and Mayannah look at Rosemary/Rosalind, surprised with her change in accent and body language.*
Mayannah is fascinated . . . the earlier misunderstanding about Rosemary's name is beginning to make sense.)

ANI: I thought you were having so much fun, Rosie.
ROSEMARY/ROSALIND: Rosalind. It's *Rosalind*.
ANI: Rosalind?
ROSEMARY/ROSALIND: Do I look like Rosie?
ANI: Uh—*yeah*!?
ROSEMARY/ROSALIND: Death, cremation, the police . . . why are you forcing me to think about things I don't want to think about? Don't you realize every word you say ricochets in my head—

colliding with all the other crap—making things worse in there for everybody?

ANI: What's going on? Is she, like, the entertainment?

ROSEMARY/ROSALIND: Oh, wouldn't you like to know? You have no idea: the traffic, the chatter, the mind-boggling soap opera chaos in there.

MAYANNAH *(Sotto to Ani, fascinated)*: It's like she put on someone else's eyes . . .

ANI: Okay, what is this? What are you trying to do to me? You into make-believe? Telling stories and lies? What are you—a Turk?

ROSEMARY/ROSALIND: Oh why don't you just take your Armenian paranoia and shove it?

ANI: You're making me, oh, a tad nervous, okay? I like to have something firm under my feet when I—

ROSEMARY/ROSALIND: Maybe a little anecdote will help. One night, one of the kids Rosemary sits for, Rosemary says to her, "It's past your bedtime, Courtney, you have to be in bed," and Courtney scrunches up her face and goes, "I know it's past my bedtime . . . but my brainpeople say I could stay up late if I want." And that word gave Rosemary the chills. Because she knows, down in the underbelly of her heart, that that word— "brainpeople"—perfectly captures this feeling she has about herself . . . this nauseous, free-floating mental achy feeling . . . that she's had since the politics started . . . since the knocks on her door at midnight . . . this feeling she can't describe to anyone but that pervades everything she does.

ANI *(Getting it)*: Oh my God.

ROSEMARY/ROSALIND: So, Mayannah, if a tiger ate Rosemary . . . would she inherit all the voices in her head? Would she know all her brainpeople? Will she remember all the screams? The darkness? And when Rosemary eats her, this delicious tiger on this plate . . . will she enter her mind?

ANI *(Trying to put it all together)*: So which one is Rosemary?

ROSEMARY/ROSALIND: *This* is Rosemary: since the day they let her stumble out of that hell in mental tatters, the only job she can get is walking dogs. Taking care of other people's babies. Anything low and servile, involving lots of shit and crying you want to pay slave wages for, she's your girl. That's the level of her self-respect! That's how much they took away from her in there!

(Trying not to get upset; to Mayannah:)

Your bathroom?

MAYANNAH *(Pointing)*: Left at the stuffed tiger.

(Rosemary/Rosalind exits to the offstage bathroom. Ani turns to Mayannah.)

ANI: A total fucked-up, one-woman circus just walked out of this room.

MAYANNAH: Yes. But don't you get it, Ani—she's so *porous* . . .

ANI: I get it and it's not for me, thanks. Mayannah, it's been—*wow*. Truly. But, you know, between the sirens and the tiger meat and Sybil in the next room . . . you need to tell your driver to take me home.

MAYANNAH: Home? What?

ANI: Yes. I don't care about the curfew. Or how many points they're going to take from me.

MAYANNAH: But you haven't touched your food. That's part of the deal. At least have the tiger meat—

ANI: But I don't even know why I'm here. Maybe this was all a mistake. I don't care how much money you're giving me. I'll find another way to leave this country!

MAYANNAH: Ani! Do you know how much I paid those hunters to track down this tiger? The number of embassies I bribed to get the carcass into my kitchen?

ANI: Too bad I don't seem to care.

MAYANNAH: But it's my anniversary dinner. The most important night of the year for me.

ANI: Look, it's hard enough for me to put myself in space when that space is mine. I don't go out, I work alone. I design and make—these—amazing little dresses for little girls—one-of-a-kind little works of art that no one wants to buy this year. So I don't have a lot of contact with other people. I really thought this might be fun, try out a few ideas, talk about Socrates!

MAYANNAH: But this is my yearly ritual: the meat, the blood, the strangers, and the crazy hope I invest.

ANI: But I don't even know what you're celebrating. You never told us.

(Beat.)

MAYANNAH: It's hunger. Hunger is why we're here.

ANI: Oh, that's not creepy—or vague!

MAYANNAH: *Mira*, I'll double the offer . . . two hundred thousand, cash, tonight . . . just sit down and eat your dinner.

ANI: Two hundred thousand? In cash?

MAYANNAH: This isn't going to be like the other years . . . I'm not going to let everything fall apart. I'm not going to scare everyone away. I don't care what it costs me.

ANI: You'd really make it two hundred?

MAYANNAH: I can do everything better. Just let me start over. Music!

(Mayannah goes to a record player. Music plays: an old bolero. Mayannah starts to dance.)

What kind of hostess am I? Letting everything get so morbid. *Life's* what's important tonight. Let's talk about life! Let's talk about love!

ANI: Let's talk about two hundred thousand dollars!

(Mayannah beckons to Ani and she goes to her. Mayannah holds Ani and they slow-dance together.)

Okay, life sounds good. So the parents are dead, huh?

MAYANNAH: Yes—but in life they were so in love, you couldn't be in the room with them when they got, you know, *that way*. In life my father was a big success in television.

ANI: Television? Really?

MAYANNAH: My Papi was seen and loved by millions. But that was before all the news programs had their balls cut off.

ANI: Seen? Your father was on the air?

MAYANNAH: Remember when they used to have international news? He did those. So I was told by La Doña. You see, I have facts about my parents but no memories . . .

ANI: What time was your father on the air?

MAYANNAH: Twice every day.

ANI: At six and eleven?

MAYANNAH: At six and eleven! How did you know?

ANI: Now you're just fucking with me.

MAYANNAH: Were you a fan? But he died before you were born. For sure, if you saw him, though, he would've driven you crazy.

ANI: Stop saying things like that!

MAYANNAH: Made Mami so jealous! La Doña told me that, in Puerto Rico, my parents loved to take long walks along the beach together. They touched each other in shameless ways, in full view of the birds and joggers! La Doña says my parents were obsessed with tigers. She says they read Borges and Kipling to me every night, spoke about tigers in whispers, and understood them in some weird, amazing way.

(Beat.)

She says my parents died together. In India. They had an accident. I was eight. That's something you don't forget. I just don't know why I forgot so many other things about them. You know how much money I'd pay to remember one thing about my parents that's all mine? That doesn't come to me predigested from a bunch of overpaid freaks who don't give a shit about me? Who never ask me if I was happy!

ANI: I'm sorry, Mayannah, that's sad, and you should see a qualified professional about that—

MAYANNAH *(Looking at Ani's hands)*: God, I love your hands, Ani . . . that was the first thing I noticed about you, the hands . . .

ANI: —but the fact that your father was on TV doing news at six and eleven freaks me out a bit because the man I was in love with—

MAYANNAH: In photos of Mami . . . her hands are exactly yours. So soft. So white! La Doña says Papi was amused by Mami's white skin. He joked that the glare made him blind. So he called her "La Blanquita." It's Spanish for "The White Girl."

(Ani pulls away from Mayannah.)

ANI: Can you shut up about this now?

MAYANNAH: I'm sorry . . . I talk about them so much because I didn't know them.

ANI: But "The White Girl" . . . that's my nickname . . .

(Rosemary/Rosalind enters from the bathroom. She's changed personalities and has become Rosemary/Roxie, a happy-go-lucky agreeable hippy.)

ROSEMARY/ROXIE: I really, really understand you, Mayannah, and I really, really support you.

ANI: Oh God, who's *this* one?

MAYANNAH: You do, Rosalind? Thank you!

ROSEMARY/ROXIE: Meet Roxie! And unlike some people who shall remain nameless, Roxie wants to hear all about your good old Papi.

MAYANNAH: Well, uhm, there was Taino Indian in him.

ROSEMARY/ROXIE: Then he must've been dark, like me!

ANI: Dark?

MAYANNAH: Yes, he was so "Indio," Mami's racist family didn't like him. So the day after they got married, they fled Puerto Rico for Los Angeles.

ROSEMARY/ROXIE: I love L.A.!

MAYANNAH: La Doña says it was hard for Mami at first, but Papi's pure green eyes reminded her of the Caribbean.

ROSEMARY/ROXIE: My eyes are green and pure!

ANI: That's it. Your eyes are green? I love green eyes, babe, and that ain't green.

ROSEMARY/ROXIE: They're a little green, you bitchy lady person, so go fuck yourself even.

ANI: I got a better idea, why don't I go over there and kick your ass?

ROSEMARY/ROXIE: No! Do you know who you're talking to?

ANI: It's anyone's guess, Roxie, Rosie, Roseface, Rosamundo, Rose Bud, Rosa Parks—!

(Rosemary/Roxie is so stressed by this onslaught, she changes personalities, becoming Rosemary/Rose, a furious, intelligent, powerful woman from the inner city.)

ROSEMARY/ROSE: My name is *Rose*, and I gotta question for you. What makes you crazy? You got any idea, Ani? Sweet, sad Ani . . . named after the sad, dead city that don't exist? *Love* makes you crazy.

(To Mayannah:)

The death of a parent makes you crazy.

(Slight beat.)

Sometimes an entire people go crazy. When you change the definition of simple words. When the abhorrent becomes familiar. When the absurd is routine. And no one seems to know the difference. Or if they know the difference, they don't talk about it, they're silent and that silence makes us crazy.

(Slight beat.)

For Rosemary? It started with the housing project she was born into. The dog shit in the hallways, the airshafts where people dumped old trash, rum bottles, unwanted babies. It was the cockroaches that seemed to live in colonies under her eyelids. The young people—her childhood friends—who died of diseases reserved for the old. It was watching the cops burst into the living room to beat the shit out of her father. It was being driven insane by lottery numbers that never hit. Winter mornings so cold she was afraid her ass would stick to the frozen toilet seat and she'd rip her skin when she stood up and she'd have a toilet-shaped scar on her ass the rest of her life. It was the sick feeling that in the tenements and projects where she was raised—and where she'll probably die a lonely, miserable death that will never make the headlines—the rules are different than they are for all the rest of the world.

(Beat.)

It was the day she rebelled against this silence. And she took to the streets. With her teacher and friends. And they shouted, "Eat the rich! Eat the rich!"—and the rich rolled out their private armies, clutching their wooden clubs and toxic gas. And they captured her. They put her in a cell . . . they put her in a cell . . . they put her in a . . .

(Rosemary/Rose changes personalities, becoming Rosemary/ Roz, a bookish, stuck-up intellectual with a pretentious accent.)

ROSEMARY/ROZ: . . . Sell your books! Write what you know! So I write about the mind and its wonderful adaptability. Ah, the mind . . . the more pressure, the more stress, instead of cracking like an egg, it gets more creative, more elastic and lucid and fertile, freer and freer to do whatever it needs to survive. I wrote three books on this! Prize winners!

MAYANNAH *(Confused)*: Books?

(Before Rosemary/Roz can respond, she changes personalities, becoming Rosemary/Rosa, an unforgiving, hungry, feral, hyperactive woman.)

ROSEMARY/ROSA: *Fuck* books! They *starve* me! There's never any food when I'm around!

(Rosemary/Rosa tears into the food, eating as fast as she can.)

It's their little power game. Hoarding the food, the light, the air. Rosie's the worst. Dublin slut! Always hogging the time and attention, like she's hot shit! But the others aren't much better. Rosalind is a compulsive narcissist. Roz, who you just met, ignores us because she has delusions of grandeur. PS her writing blows. Roseanne doesn't speak to Rose. The Teacher thinks we're idiots. And everyone's worried about Tom!

ANI *(To Mayannah)*: Who's Tom?

ROSEMARY/ROSA: You leave Tom out of this, lady!

ANI: You dragged Tom into this!

ROSEMARY/ROSA: Tom's my favorite, my angel. I'm gonna save some food for Tom!

(She eats.)

What the others don't know is there's no controlling a force of nature like me. They think I'm something Rosemary made up in the dark, screaming, lonely hole of her cell. But I'm as natural and real and here as this awesomely tasty pile of flesh on my plate.

(Laughs bitterly.)

You see, I'm the custodian. The caretaker of our little mental family. You try being that. Guardian and witness to her life. Since the day of her release, I've had to watch her scratch and scramble month after month in some isolated shoebox in a building full of freaks. Watching her sleep with the landlord for a small discount on the rent. And I'm the only one—of the hundreds of us—who bothers to talk to her. Who whispers to her, night after night: "What happened to your courage, girl? Your pride? You've got to get back on your feet! The cause needs you! You could be a hero!" Does she listen to me? No!

(Ani is clearly upset by this deluge of personalities.)

MAYANNAH: We'll call it three hundred thousand.

ANI *(Can't believe it; in Armenian)*: Ah-mah!

ROSEMARY/ROSA: Yeah, she had it bad in there . . . it was one continuous nightmare and thank God she's forgotten it . . . the sensory deprivation and beatings . . . the serial rapes . . . but lots of others suffered worse and they didn't *crumble* like she did. That's what pisses me off: she *broke*. She lets the nightmares win time and time and—

(Rosemary/Rosa changes personalities, becoming Rosemary/Teacher, a benign, patient, older woman with a Southern accent.)

ROSEMARY/TEACHER: Time is like a prison, students. That's the lesson for all of you today. They torture the person in the cell next to yours, and you hear Time removing eyes and replacing them with marbles covered with cataracts. Removing ears and replacing them with shells stuffed with cotton. You hear knees being worn to the bone. Nerves plugged with mucus. Arthritis sprayed on the hands. Blood to the sex organs diverted to the thick, blue, intestine-shaped veins in the legs. Memories segregated into darker and deeper little rooms in the mind, as all the signs that tell you how to find those memories are covered in cobwebs and dust. The prisoner being tortured by Time in the cell next to yours doesn't scream. All you hear is the clocklike beat of torture instruments. And all you can do in your cell is wait for Time to finish with your neighbor and come for you. And you wait so long that on the day it comes to get you, you don't realize Time's already had its way with you—and you never even noticed.

(Beat.)

What? What do you want to say? Don't you understand it's rude to interrupt?

(Beat.)

Two minutes, Tom! You can come out and say—

(Rosemary/Teacher turns into Rosemary/Tom, a frightened little boy with a slight stutter.)

ROSEMARY/TOM: Hi! Check it, I gotta t-talk fast 'cause they don't let me have a lot of t-time in Life! That's 'cause I'm such a prize fuck-up and I never get no chance to fix my shit, I mean, I just can't rewind my life and h-hope to do it better, can I?

MAYANNAH: Maybe you can.

ROSEMARY/TOM *(Not listening)*: So when I get out, I'm so lost, I can't do anything right and it m-makes me so sad and I can't stand myself no more—and I just wanna cut myself—bad.

(Rosemary/Tom grabs one of the knives on the table and puts it to her arm.
Ani and Mayannah go to her.)

MAYANNAH: Rosemary, don't!

ANI: Holy shit!

(Rosemary/Tom holds the sharp blade against her skin.)

ROSEMARY/TOM: Hey, I know Rosemary's just like me. That's how come I just love her so much and I always fight the others, defending Rosemary—"G-give her a chance," I tell 'em. "Rosemary's really trying to get on with her life, you guys!" Man, Rosemary's so soft. Those pretty brown eyes. I kiss her when no one's looking. I'm not supposed to. She has dreams, and I watch them like movies, and they make me laugh. I don't get one thing—how come Rosemary knows Rosie and Rosa and all them others . . . but she don't know Tom . . . she don't know I'm here and how bad I wanna love her and heal her and marry her and start a family.

(Rosemary/Tom puts the knife down and weeps. Mayannah quickly takes the knife. Ani crosses herself.
Rosemary/Teacher and Rosemary/Tom talk to each other.)

ROSEMARY/TEACHER: Time to go to bed, Tom.

ROSEMARY/TOM: But I'm still hungry. And my brainpeople say I can stay up late if I want!

ROSEMARY/TEACHER: Nice try, but the lights are going out on you, Tom.

ROSEMARY/TOM: I hate the dark in here . . . all those voices scare me! Rosalind's so mean!

ROSEMARY/TEACHER: I love you, baby . . . don't cry.

ROSEMARY/TOM: Don't leave me alone, Teacher . . .

(Rosemary/Teacher/Tom struggles to change personalities . . . it's an intense struggle, the most violent we've seen. Finally she changes personalities, becoming default-Rosemary, the original personality out of which all the others were born, a deeply wounded soul just trying to survive.)

ROSEMARY: *. . . Oh my God . . . my head . . .*

(Rosemary looks around . . . sees Mayannah and Ani as if for the first time.)

. . . oh my God, where am I?

(Mayannah approaches Rosemary cautiously.)

MAYANNAH: My house.

ROSEMARY: You. I remember you. You—invited me to your mansion, on some street only sheiks and kingpins can afford . . . Saturday night.

(Mayannah recognizes her.)

MAYANNAH: Are you *her*? . . .

ROSEMARY: Does that mean it's Saturday right now?!

MAYANNAH: Ani, I think this is the one I met that night—the one I invited. It's Rosemary.

ANI: Yay.

ROSEMARY: Oh my God, I've lost three whole days, haven't I? I've never lost three days in a row before. What have I been doing all this time?

MAYANNAH: We don't know, Rosemary, we just met you!

ROSEMARY: Oh God, this is bad. You know how much trouble I could have caused in three days?

(Checks her body out.)

No new scars, no bruises, nothing broken . . . okay, that's encouraging . . .

(To Mayannah and Ani:)

Did I steal anything, break anything, sleep with anyone you know?

(Quick; looks at them.)

Please don't judge me. You don't know me. You don't know what I go through. The blackouts . . . they were only minutes in the beginning . . . now they're days. That's a disaster!

(To herself:)

Focus, Ro. Don't spin out of control. First things first. You're not home. Deal with that. Find out where you are.

(To Mayannah:)

Uhm, where are we?

MAYANNAH: Downtown. Flower Street.

ROSEMARY: That's miles from me. How did I get here?

MAYANNAH: I sent an armored limo to pick you up.

ROSEMARY *(Starts to remember)*: Dinner party . . . a hundred thousand bucks . . . you said you always ask two strangers . . .

(To Ani:)

Are you the other one?

(Afraid, Ani doesn't answer.)

Have I offended you? Whatever I said to you before, I'm sorry—it wasn't me—

(Noticing the table.)

Oh my God, did I eat this shit? Excuse me, but except for white meat, I'm a strict vegetarian!

ANI: Wait'll she finds out it's not pork.

ROSEMARY: This isn't funny. You just don't know what it's like for me. I wake up with ticket stubs in my pocket to places I never went to. On the street, women I don't know slap my face for sleeping with guys I never met. At home I open my diary and the words are in someone else's handwriting—the craziest shit you ever heard.

ANI: I bet that's true.

ROSEMARY: Oh my God, how many of them did you meet? All of them are imposters, no matter what they say. And each one, when they come out, they think they're the center, the essence of me . . . but they're not . . . there's only one, only me . . . I am Rosemary!

(From a pocket, she takes out a wallet full of pictures, which she shows to Ani and Mayannah.)

That's me at eight. The projects where I grew up. My best friend Tom just before he died in police custody. My favorite teacher who taught me not to believe the lies they tell you. This girl I met in a bar called Dublin—she really loved to have a good time. Look: a drawing of me by Rosario. She draws me with horns and a tail because she hates me. They *all* hate me. They've tried to kill me. They've put rat poison in my food. You know how many times I've had my stomach pumped? They've cut my wrists. And I'm just a real average girl who just wants a little normal happiness and no more drama, no more politics . . . there was a knock at the door at midnight, something happened. I can't remember now . . . and now I just want maybe someone to love me and make a family with me some day . . . believe me . . .

(Rosemary suddenly, like whiplash, changes personalities, becoming Rosemary/Rosario, a fiercely violent, malignant woman.)

ROSEMARY/ROSARIO: —when I say the one who says she's the real Rosemary is a liar. A *killer*. She's wanted for all those horrible murders in the projects. Mutilations. She's the one the police are looking for tonight. Don't trust her! HIDE THOSE KNIVES!

(Like whiplash again, Rosemary/Rosario changes personalities becoming default Rosemary. She looks at the frightened Ani and Mayannah.)

ROSEMARY: —God, what are you looking at? What's wrong? What just happened?

(Beat.)

You don't believe me, do you? You think I'm one of them telling you stories. You don't believe I'm really here—

ROSEMARY/ROSIE: You're not here!

ROSEMARY/ROXIE: You're not here!

ROSEMARY/ROSE: You're not here!

ROSEMARY/ROSARIO: YOU WERE NEVER HERE!

(Rosemary changes personalities, becoming Rosemary/Rosalie, a woman so uncountably old and slow, she appears almost comatose.

Silence as Ani and Mayannah look at Rosemary/Rosalie, waiting for her to reveal herself.)

ROSEMARY/ROSALIE: My.

(Silence.

Rosemary/Rosalie barely moves or breathes. Ani and May-annah get closer to her, apprehensive.)

MAYANNAH: Hello?

(No response from Rosemary/Rosalie.)

ANI: She's dead, right?

(Mayannah touches Rosemary/Rosalie's forehead, and quickly pulls her hand away.)

MAYANNAH: Ay! Hot!

ANI *(Putting knives away)*: What's going on with her?

MAYANNAH: It's like she overheated . . . she shut down.

ANI: I'm ready to shut down.

ROSEMARY/ROSALIE: Mind.

MAYANNAH: She's going to be fine. I think she's just resting.

ANI: Are you sure we don't need your doctor? Maybe he's got a straitjacket?

MAYANNAH: Poor thing. You wanted to know what the soul is like? This one's in shreds because of what they did to her . . .

(Mayannah gently strokes Rosemary/Rosalie's hair.)

ANI: How can you be so calm? You know what you brought into your house?

MAYANNAH: I do.

ANI: And that's cool with you?

MAYANNAH: It is.

ANI: So is that why you picked her? Because she's a village?

MAYANNAH: I picked her for her lovely eyes.

(Ani is at her emotional wit's end. She rubs her tired eyes.)

ANI: So *why*? Out of this endless army of screwed-up people that night in front of the bar . . . why did you have to pick me?

130

MAYANNAH: I told you.

ANI: Yeah, my hands. "Lovely eyes, lovely hands." That explains the whole thing.

MAYANNAH: Some more rum?

ANI: I mean, for all I know you and Rosemary are working together to play some wicked sick game on me.

MAYANNAH: Why would we do that?

ROSEMARY/ROSALIE: Has.

ANI: Who needs a reason to be cruel anymore? It's sport. It's fun. It's: let's see how much we can get away with.

MAYANNAH: Ani, that's a little paranoid—

ANI: You're the one with the fucking army! And the naked Jesuses!

MAYANNAH: But I've given you no reason to—

ANI: Don't you think this happens to me all the time? That I'm victim to little bouts of mental cruelty a dozen times a day? Don't you think I feel the creepy little war going on out there between the weak and the strong?

MAYANNAH: But we can make something with the three of us that's real and healthy—

ANI: Healthy? I haven't slept in days. I'm so alone, I'm free-falling. People and the words they say don't connect. I don't recognize the world I was born into. Everyone's got *secrets* but no one's got *privacy*. And soon as it gets dark, the soldiers crawl out like vampires and make things worse.

MAYANNAH: But with me and Rosemary, in this house, you don't have to be alone.

ANI: But something in me was stolen. I'm beyond alone. I'm less than myself.

MAYANNAH: But don't you feel potential between us? To be more than friends? More than lovers?

ANI: Mayannah, I came here for money. Not to be friends. Money. Please, give me the money so I can go.

MAYANNAH: I can't.

ANI *(Trying not to get emotional)*: Look, I really need to get out of this country. To live in some village somewhere . . . with mud bricks and donkeys . . . not just because of what this country's become, which is bad enough, heartbreaking enough . . . I need to go so I can forget *him*. To be where everything doesn't remind me of how stupid I've been . . .

MAYANNAH: Say it with me: men are *mierda*.

ANI: Men are *kak udogh*! Shit-eaters! And when you hear what this particular shit-eater did to me, you'll give me the money, I know you will. I won't have to eat that tiger meat to get my money and freedom.

MAYANNAH *(Sympathetic)*: Ani . . .

ANI *(Trying not to cry)*: The thing is, when he turned on me . . . he didn't just take himself away . . . he took pieces of all my important organs, slices of my memories, half my prayers . . . and it started off so good, you know?

MAYANNAH: Always does.

ANI: I can't remember the first time I saw Miguel.

MAYANNAH: My father's name!

ANI: I was channel-surfing. It was a sea of faces. So many of those TV faces are plastic, like the opposite of attractive . . . but there he was suddenly. I couldn't take my eyes off him. He wasn't plastic or perfect but that's what made him perfect. I started seeing him right away. At six, I'd turn on the TV and get in bed. At first I'd close my eyes and just listened to him. I wouldn't give myself the pleasure of looking at his face . . . just to heighten the suspense and joy. Then I'd open my eyes to watch his mouth form those words, those lips around those orb-shaped vowels, and I'd get so horny. By the time I took care of business, his broadcast was over and I turned him off until eleven, and it would start all over again.

ROSEMARY/ROSALIE: Been.

ANI: Why did everything have to turn to shit? All I wanted was to look at him, listen to him. There was all this endless stuff between us. It was the only time I understood what "infinity" meant. Like there was an infinite number of choices between us, an infinite number of ways to be happy. And for one sweet month, I thought I was pregnant! I had dreams of a daughter with wild, dark hair, like yours. I made all these great little dresses for her. But she was just a dream.

MAYANNAH: A dream.

ANI: Then one night at six, I turned on the TV . . . and he didn't say anything . . . he just sat there, staring at me. I didn't know what to do, so I hit the side of the TV—and he "woke up" and started his broadcast. Okay, weird. But then he did the same thing at eleven—except this time he had a scary, annoyed reaction when I hit the TV. Same thing happened the next day! I got so freaked, I changed to another channel! I mean, I can't be in a relationship, even if the sex is great, if I'm scared of the other person, you know? I'm not crazy for thinking that, right? Then I woke up one morning . . . it was that first week of martial law . . . and my TV was already on! And there he was. Just staring at me. And I lost it. I started screaming: "Leave me alone! You're too crazy for me! It's over between us!" I was walking up and down, foaming at the mouth, and that's when I saw his eyes following me. Well, I unplugged the TV and threw it out the window.

ROSEMARY/ROSALIE: Ruined.

ANI: A few nights later I was in the only government-approved bar in my neighborhood, drowning my sorrows, and I didn't notice the TV. It was eleven. I was the only woman. The streets were quiet except for the armored vehicles. The place was full of cigarette smoke—and tension. Because no one knew what was going to happen. When the news came on, I thought they were going to show that woman who set herself on fire in front of the Supreme Court to protest the canceled election and the arrest and torture of the dissidents—but, no—it was him. With a really nasty look on his face. I'm screaming: "You can't hurt me anymore, motherfucker!" He smirked! The sound was off but the captions were on . . . so I started reading. You know what I read? The fucker was reading my diary! Hello! On the air! All the men in the bar got, like, riveted to my sordid life story. To all the ways love turns to shit. To all the creative abuse men have turned into art forms. To all the tricks I used just to survive. My face turned white from dread, then red from anger. And the men standing around me, who were learning all the dark secrets of a single woman's mind, they were hooked. Some took notes. Some called buddies on their cells. All laughed at my dumb, pathetic life. When they saw my face change colors, they figured out it was me they were reading about. All their eyes locked on me . . . this piece of nervous meat who had the balls to think she knew how a man's great mind worked . . . those eyes started to *strip* me, Mayannah . . . to pull off my clothes, then my skin . . . then all the inner goo, down to the electricity in my nerves, to my soul, which they tried to see with their X-ray eyes, reducing me to nothing, to air, to moisture, to nothing. When they knew everything they needed to know about me, I didn't need to exist.

(Beat.)

I left the bar crying and grabbed a streetlamp so I wouldn't fall over and that's when a stranger with morbid eyes and black hair walked up to me and knew I'd be too weak and lonely to say no to her beauty, her wealth and her invitation to dinner on Saturday night . . .

ROSEMARY/ROSALIE: By.

(Beat.)

ANI: I used to look to a lover to reflect myself back to me, to describe reality to me: I'd know about my soul that way; I'd have some idea of my own intelligence and value because of the dented mirrors my lover held up, and I'd look into them and search for the truth and try to understand what my soul was made of. This man taught me that all these mirrors lie, Mayannah. They lie.

(Mayannah is moved by Ani's story and she holds her.)

MAYANNAH: Oh, Ani.

ROSEMARY/ROSALIE: Poverty.

(Grateful for the unexpected comfort, Ani holds her tight.)

ANI: Now, when I'm in bed . . . and think about love and what it does to my heart . . . I can feel . . . my heart changing shape. First it's a pyramid, then it's round and hard like a fist, then soft and gooey like a giant amoeba—never valentine-shaped or pretty or pink. And it always feels way too big for my body. And all I want is to take my big, freakish heart and get out of this country and go into the world and find a love so good and real, it will make my heart change into a true valentine shape. But my heart always seems about to collapse under its own weight and I'm sure I'm going to die from its crazy hunger and its unbearable ability to feel. Does that make any sense?

(Beat.)

MAYANNAH *(Soft, sympathetic)*: Sí, mi amor, sí.

(Mayannah goes off and comes back with a black leather bag. She goes to Ani with the bag.)

ROSEMARY/ROSALIE: My.
ANI: What's that?
MAYANNAH: Enough money to get you out of this country forever. What happens to your heart after that, Ani . . . I don't know.

(Mayannah hands the bag to Ani.
   Ani, almost shocked, opens the bag and looks at all the money.)

ANI: Wow—this is mine? I don't have to do anything for it?
MAYANNAH: You've gone through enough . . . just take the money and go home. I'll watch over her—them—until they're okay to go.
ANI: I'm really done?
MAYANNAH: If you want to go now, I'll call the driver.

(Ani looks at Mayannah with admiration.)

ROSEMARY/ROSALIE: Mind.

ANI: Someone who keeps their word. That's new in my life. I guess maybe I was wrong about you.

MAYANNAH: I'm sorry we never got to be friends.

ANI: I'm sorry I was so high-maintenance tonight. I'm Armenian, you know.

MAYANNAH *(Smiles)*: Yeah, I know.

ROSEMARY/ROSALIE: Has.

(Mayannah sadly starts to clear the table, blowing out the black candles, etc.)

ANI: This totally ruins your plan for tonight, doesn't it? This whole thing you do every year. I mean, what did you expect me and Rosemary to do?

MAYANNAH: It doesn't matter now. It was stupid . . .

(Ani looks at her, compassionate.)

ANI: Well, I think it's cool you wanted me and Rosemary to be your friends. I know what it's like to live without any love. I hope that changes for you. Maybe you'll meet a guy sometime? Invite one to dinner instead of a couple of crazy women?

MAYANNAH *(The meat)*: I'll have to throw this all out . . .

ANI *(Trying to connect)*: Have you ever loved a man like I did? Crazy like that?

MAYANNAH *(Trying not to get emotional)*: My mind has been . . . .

ROSEMARY/ROSALIE: Been.

MAYANNAH: There are forms of love I just don't know and don't think I'll ever know.

ANI: I know all the shitty forms. Like I have a PhD in it.

MAYANNAH: If I want a man's love . . . well, este, it's a good thing I'm filthy rich.

ANI: You pay for men?

ROSEMARY/ROSALIE: Ruined.

MAYANNAH: Men, boys, women, groups on tour. El Doctor checks them out. Says it's good for me to do it as much as I can. But I have rules. I never have the same person more than once. No names.

ANI: Isn't that—like—impersonal?

MAYANNAH: I'm not supposed to enjoy it, Ani. Sometimes I put nails in my bed. I once made love to a man in a coffin. I had sex with a woman on her dying day. I felt her final breath on my cheek—and I came.

ANI: Just when I'm starting to like you, you have to say shit like that . . .

MAYANNAH: I can only have sex that takes me down and away and far from all this, where I can smell the dirt in my grave and feel the rough chill of my tombstone.

(Silence.)

ANI: Mayannah? Can you come back to the living, please?

MAYANNAH *(Smiles)*: You're funny.

ANI: No, you're funny.

ROSEMARY/ROSALIE: By.

MAYANNAH: Where do you go—even if it's just in your dreams—you and your man?

ANI: I see us on the beach . . . the waves make, like, liquid sucking sounds . . . and we touch each other in broad daylight right in front of . . .

ANI AND MAYANNAH: . . . the birds and joggers.

ANI: The trouble is . . . he made me think the only true, good, free, perfect love is the love you imagine.

MAYANNAH: Because he broke something in you.

ANI: Is that why I miss him so much?

MAYANNAH: It's not him you miss. What you miss is yourself, unbroken.

(Agreeing with this, Ani nods yes, tries not to cry.)

ROSEMARY/ROSALIE: Poverty.

ANI: Yes. I do. So much. You should've seen me as a little girl. I was so tough. So cool.

MAYANNAH: I was that kind of girl, too.

(Beat.)

ANI: Maybe we could've been friends. You're a nice person.

MAYANNAH *(Surprised)*: You think so?

ANI: Well, a little too gothic for your own good, and maybe I would redecorate in here a little . . . but, yeah.

ROSEMARY/ROSALIE: My.

MAYANNAH: That night, in front of the bar . . . the one day in the year I go out, and I love it because it feels like freedom, and that feeling scares me in a good way . . . I saw so many people; I rejected them all . . . except for Rosemary who had these haunted eyes I couldn't forget . . . and there was something in your hands, Ani. Like I knew them before.

ANI: Like from another life?

MAYANNAH: Hands that put me to bed. Hands that held copies of Borges and Kipling. Hands that worked so hard for my future.

ANI: A better life?

MAYANNAH: A much better life. Yes.

ANI: How do you find that? A better life? A completely new way to live? Do you have to do like Rosemary and be so many people maybe one of them will survive and be happy?

ROSEMARY/ROSALIE: Mind.

(Mayannah takes a shot of rum and looks at Ani, heartened by Ani's statement that they could have been friends.)

MAYANNAH: Maybe we could do that. If we can be friends . . . maybe it's not too late to do what you just said.

ANI: Turn into Rosemary?

MAYANNAH: Find a new way to live. Really live, you know?

ANI: Out of this country?

MAYANNAH: Away from the staff and the soldiers—

ANI: —and the past—

MAYANNAH: —and the animal meat. What do you think? You and me and all the Rosemarys!

ANI: Could get crowded.

MAYANNAH: We'll live in a big house, in a cool, obscure country. We'll go topless all day and cook big meals together!

ANI: No endangered species!

MAYANNAH: You could find love. Rosemary could find peace and wholeness. I could wear another color besides black. I could travel to India and kill tigers in person. I'll finally finish this madness. And we could start right now. We don't have to wait for anyone's permission. I'm a goddamn grown woman. And I have money.

ROSEMARY/ROSALIE: Has.

(Mayannah fingers the diamond necklaces around her neck.)

MAYANNAH: I could sell these rocks—or use them like dollar bills. I can bribe the driver. We can flirt with the soldiers.

ANI: I know how to flirt.

MAYANNAH: We'll buy new IDs on the black market and start our lives tonight, Ani. Yes?

ANI: Yes.

MAYANNAH: Yes!

ROSEMARY/ROSALIE: Been.

(Mayannah goes to a telephone and picks it up.
Another series of eerie police, fire and emergency sirens—closer this time, louder. Mayannah listens, immobile.)

ANI: May . . . ?

ROSEMARY/ROSALIE: Ruined.

(Mayannah doesn't move as she listens to the sirens. Worried, Ani goes to the window and looks out.)

ANI: It's okay . . . they're going somewhere else.

(Mayannah puts the phone down.)

MAYANNAH: What do I think I'm doing?
ANI: It's okay—we can go.
MAYANNAH: I didn't go the first time . . . I can't go now . . .

(Ani goes to the telephone.)

ANI: I can call the driver if you can't.
MAYANNAH: No. I can't do it. I can't go.
ANI: With all that money, we can do anything—
MAYANNAH: *Fuck* the money!

(Mayannah angrily tears the necklaces off her neck, and throws them on the floor.
   She starts tearing at her earrings and bracelets. Ani grabs Mayannah, and holds on to her, making her stop.)

ANI: What's wrong with you? Why can't you get out of this morgue? What the fuck is keeping you here?
ROSEMARY/ROSALIE: By.
MAYANNAH: Can you tell me . . . why would God curse a child, Ani?
ANI: Did God curse a child? Is that what happened to you?
ROSEMARY/ROSALIE: Poverty.
MAYANNAH: I can't look out a window or an open door without wanting to throw up.

(Ani holds her tighter.)

ANI: C'mon, stop it.

(Mayannah pulls away. Wipes her eyes.)

MAYANNAH: Every room I look into . . . it's the same room . . . the same thing happens there.
ANI: What room?
MAYANNAH: I don't want to go in there again—
ANI: Where is the room?

MAYANNAH: I said I don't want to go in there! I don't want to see it anymore!

ANI: If you don't go back into that room, you're never going to leave it. Is that what you want? To be stuck? So next year you can go out and find two more pathetic losers to freak out? And the year after? When does all this end, May?

ROSEMARY/ROSALIE: My.

MAYANNAH: Is it supposed to end?

ANI: Only if you don't want to wallow in this sickness all your life. Is that what you really want? What about that new way to live?

MAYANNAH: I don't know if I can tell you.

ANI: If not us, who are you going to tell? That staff you never talk to? The soldiers? The police who tortured poor Rosemary? Your dead mother and father? They can't hear you. They can't take care of you. I can hear you, though, I can.

(Mayannah's entire body seems to shake as the memories come back, a struggle between past and present.)

MAYANNAH: It's a church. It's a church, Ani!

ROSEMARY/ROSALIE: Mind.

(Mayannah speaks as much to herself as to Ani.)

MAYANNAH: It's a church.

ANI: I'm getting . . . that it's a church.

MAYANNAH: An old church in Puerto Rico.

ANI: Make me see it. Take me there.

(Beat.)

MAYANNAH: The three of us are in the church. It started off so good.

ANI: Always does.

ROSEMARY/ROSALIE: Has.

MAYANNAH: Papi made me laugh. He cooked my favorite eggs that morning.

ANI: Good old Papi.

MAYANNAH: It's my first time in this old church. They were married here. I'm so nervous, I need to pee. I'm so little, I have to look up to see everything.

(Takes invisible hands.)

Mami was here. Papi here.
ROSEMARY/ROSALIE: Been.
MAYANNAH: Holding hands.

(A little girl's command:)

Holding hands.
ANI: Holding hands.
MAYANNAH: Everyone's looking at us. That's because my Papi drives women crazy. Young women whisper his name as he walks by—
ANI: Miguel!
MAYANNAH: They say it with such heat.
ANI *(With heat)*: Miguel!
MAYANNAH: La Blanquita doesn't like it.
ANI: But you love it, don't you?
MAYANNAH: Yes. I'm proud. I have the best Papi. But I see him only on Sundays and on TV. When he reads the international news. I always kiss the TV when he's on. And he always smiles when I do it. He once read my poem on TV.
ANI: It all sounds so good, so perfect.
ROSEMARY/ROSALIE: Ruined.
MAYANNAH: It's the day of my First Communion. The three of us hold hands up the aisle. Ay, the smells. Camellias, "Old Spice," "Paradise." My new black shoes are tight. I'm in a long white dress Mami made by hand for me. My hair done all special. The floor creaks. The air is humid, old. In the pews, poor people, on their knees, pray to la Virgen for lottery numbers to hit, for pregnancies to end well, for husbands to stop cheating— they beg and beg for a million secular miracles. *Then I see him.*
ROSEMARY/ROSALIE: By.

MAYANNAH: He's . . . almost as big as Papi. Almost . . . naked. I'm scared. I want to pull back . . .

(Gasps.)

Then I see the blood. In front of me is a young man impaled on an upside-down sword, nailed into space. And—he's sweating; he's breathing. He's still alive. And he knows that I know. His dark eyes move—his mouth opens—he tries to say something to me.

(Points her finger.)

I scream: "Help him! Get him down from there!"

(Beat.)

My parents don't know what's wrong with me. And I don't know why everyone keeps walking past this poor, handsome young man—those strong, long muscles; those thin, hard hips—those dark eyes full of old music—his soft, fleshy mouth. And I'm the only one who can see him the way he really is. His eyes beg me to wipe his bloody face and soothe his young, mighty heart, to take him home, feed him rice and beans, put my fingers in his wounds— and eat his sorrow. I run out of the church. He haunts me all day. Even after my parents laugh at me for thinking that the huge wood crucifix in the back of the church is real. They tell all their friends what a boba I am for ruining my First Communion. That night we have dinner. Lots of meat and butter. It's pouring rain. I'm talking about a book report. My parents are excited because they're going to India to shoot pictures of tigers in the wild. This would be the first trip they'll take without me—and I'm hopping mad. And I can't stop thinking of the crucifix because I know it's a bad omen, and I try to warn them not to go to India without me and they just think I'm being childish and that's the last time I see them alive. I'm not in India to protect them and they don't come back.

ROSEMARY/ROSALIE: Poverty.

MAYANNAH: I wait by the window. Months pass. I scream for my parents, for answers. Then I just stop screaming.

(Slight beat.)

La Doña takes control of my parents' fortune. She sets up a corporation to raise me. The house is full of sad-eyed, silent staff members, dressing me, feeding me, listening to me rant and rave, trying to relate to this stunned, eight-year-old orphan. Nobody kisses me. When I start demanding some affection, La Doña tells me my parents were eaten by tigers. Only parts of their bodies were recovered. Those few bones were cremated. That ends it for me.

(Mayannah goes silent as she wipes her eyes.)

ROSEMARY/ROSALIE: My mind.

MAYANNAH: So every year I celebrate the anniversary of our last night together as a family by paying two complete strangers to have dinner with me, and serving them tiger meat.

(Ani goes to Mayannah and envelopes her maternally in her arms.)

ANI: But, Mayannah—your parents—you can't say that was your fault.

MAYANNAH: Yes! If I had just convinced them to take me . . .

ANI: That's why you're torturing yourself? You were just a child. An innocent kid.

(Mayannah pulls away from Ani, angry, stubborn, lost.)

MAYANNAH: And every year, I do everything I can to re-create that final meal: the dishes, the rum, the food. The only thing I change is the meat. But year after year, no matter what I did . . . the miracle never happened. Then I realized it can't be just any tiger. There was only one and I had to find her.

(Mayannah looks at the meat on the table.)

ROSEMARY/ROSALIE: Has been.
MAYANNAH: That's why I was so sure this year would be different. This year El Cocinero told me: "We think we've found her . . . the daughter of the tiger who ate your mother and father! We think this is her!"

(Ani looks at the table.)

ANI: This one's the daughter? That's who we're eating tonight?

(Mayannah looks closely at the tiger meat.)

ROSEMARY/ROSALIE: Ruined by.
MAYANNAH: Look at her. She's magnificent. Such a waste . . .

(Ani looks at the tiger meat, finally understanding its significance.)

That's why I asked you: are we really what we eat? And can we ever really know, Ani, what mysteries are passed down from mother to daughter?
ANI *(Quiet)*: Or *who* is.
MAYANNAH: Yes, who.
ANI: That's why we're here. To eat the past.
ROSEMARY/ROSALIE: Poverty. My.
MAYANNAH: I figured something out when the Rosemarys exploded and you talked about your love. All I wanted was to take back what the world stole from me. But now I think . . . this meal, this night, doesn't belong just to me. This is also her night— and yours.
ANI: Mine?
MAYANNAH: I can give you all the money I have . . . what will change, Ani? *Really* change. Your heart? Your place in this

dirty food chain we live in? I think tonight, Ani, it's possible, just possible, I don't know . . . but I think I can give you something more than the money you crave. I can give you, and poor Rosemary . . .

ROSEMARY/ROSALIE: Mind has been.

(Mayannah pulls out Ani's chair at the table, inviting her to sit.)

MAYANNAH: . . . a whole new life.

(Ani takes a breath, looks at Mayannah, at the meat, then sits at her place at the table. Ani picks up her fork.)

ANI *(To herself)*: A whole new life.

(Ani stabs a piece of tiger meat. She puts it in her mouth and eats it . . . an unexpected smile.)

Wow, it is good. *Khentanaleekeh!*

(Tears form in Mayannah's eyes.)

MAYANNAH: I don't know what that means—but I told you.

ROSALIE/ROSEMARY: Ruined by poverty.

(Ani hungrily eats the tiger meat. Mayannah looks at her as if expecting something to happen.
  After a few moments, Ani stops, confused.)

ANI: I don't feel anything.

(Mayannah says nothing.)

What was I supposed to feel?

MAYANNAH *(Quiet)*: I don't know exactly . . .

146

(Ani gets up from the table. Goes to the silent Mayannah, hugs and kisses her.)

ANI: It didn't work. I'm sorry. Did you really think it would?
MAYANNAH *(Beat)*: I guess I did.
ANI: Maybe it's me. Maybe I don't have magic.

(Mayannah goes to the telephone to call her driver. Ani gets up from the table.
Suddenly Rosemary/Rosalie stirs as she tries to get back to consciousness.)

ROSEMARY/ROSALIE *(Quiet)*: My—mind—has—been—ruined—by— poverty . . .

(Mayannah dials the phone.
Ani looks at Rosemary/Rosalie, not knowing what to expect of her.)

ANI: And she's back.

(Another internal struggle and Rosemary/Rosalie changes personalities becoming Rosemary/Miguel, a middle-aged, aristocratic Puerto Rican man.
Rosemary/Miguel stares at Ani a silent moment.)

ROSEMARY/MIGUEL: Blanquita? Mi amor, is that you?

(Mayannah nearly gasps when she hears this new voice. She puts the phone down.
Ani doesn't know how to respond. Is motionless, waiting. She looks at Mayannah.)

ANI: Is that—*him*?
MAYANNAH: Ay Dios mio.
ANI: Mayannah . . . a little help?

ROSEMARY/MIGUEL: You look frightened, Blanquita! My little White Girl!

ANI: Is she—? Is he—?

ROSEMARY/MIGUEL: That's your nickname, isn't it? "White Girl"?

ANI: Yes, but—

ROSEMARY/MIGUEL: What would you like to do? How do we start to trust each other?

ANI *(To Mayannah)*: I don't know what to do.

ROSEMARY/MIGUEL: May I suggest . . .

ANI *(Feeling weak, taking off her glasses)*: And I really feel weird . . .

ROSEMARY/MIGUEL: . . . that we do something . . .

ANI *(Weaker)*: I should go.

ROSEMARY/MIGUEL: . . . like *this*? . . .

(Rosemary/Miguel goes to Ani and gently kisses her. The kiss seems to send a jolt through Ani's body.

As Rosemary/Miguel kisses Ani, Mayannah gasps—not from surprise, but because it looks so familiar.)

ANI: *Oh my God . . .*

(Rosemary/Miguel goes to the necklace Mayannah had ripped off her body, picks it up, and puts it around Ani's neck. Takes down her hair.

A struggle in Ani's mind and body as she changes personalities, becoming Ani/Blanquita, a young aristocratic Puerto Rican woman.)

ROSEMARY/MIGUEL: I ask again: how do we start?

ANI/BLANQUITA: Do we take a walk, Miguel?

MAYANNAH: A walk would be perfect.

ROSEMARY/MIGUEL: A walk would be perfect!

MAYANNAH: Along a body of water.

ANI/BLANQUITA: Along a body of water.

ROSEMARY/MIGUEL: Something deep, ancient, and not too polluted.

ANI/BLANQUITA: Reminding us that we're shallow, young and a little dirty.

ROSEMARY/MIGUEL: No words for a long time.

ANI/BLANQUITA: Words would ruin it.

ROSEMARY/MIGUEL: We let the tide and the moon have their conversation.

ANI/BLANQUITA: They talk about love and attraction.

ROSEMARY/MIGUEL: They talk about gravity and moisture.

ANI/BLANQUITA: Would I stop during our walk? Would I stop in your path?

ROSEMARY/MIGUEL: And face me. Block my way.

ANI/BLANQUITA: My two strong legs slightly apart. My mouth open.

ROSEMARY/MIGUEL: The moon and the tide stop talking. They watch us. Anticipation is killing them.

ANI/BLANQUITA: I spend a long time looking at your face. Planning my move.

ROSEMARY/MIGUEL: My hands sweat.

ANI/BLANQUITA: Do I forget how I was raised? Good Catholic girl? A good family? One of the best in Puerto Rico! A reputation as long as history itself!

ROSEMARY/MIGUEL: Anticipation is killing me.

ANI/BLANQUITA: Do I forget all that and simply let your hand come down inside my legs, Miguel?

ROSEMARY/MIGUEL: ¡Ay, mi Blanquita! Yes!

ANI/BLANQUITA: And I become liquid around your finger!

ROSEMARY/MIGUEL: Not a bad way to start the day!

ANI/BLANQUITA: I want to stop you, but I can't. Everything I've been taught about men—it's all true! Pigs, all of you!

ROSEMARY/MIGUEL: ¡Gracias! Then?

ANI/BLANQUITA: Do I take hold of you? Gently? Will the birds and joggers see me?

ROSEMARY/MIGUEL: That could happen.

ANI/BLANQUITA: I'm afraid I'll be seen. Not by God—but by the staff my parents employ to spy on me! Their princess! Their prisoner! After only a moment, I let go of it!

ROSEMARY/MIGUEL: As if it were burning your hand!

ANI/BLANQUITA: It was! My God, it was!

ROSEMARY/MIGUEL: Then we go to eat. We talk about the future.

ANI/BLANQUITA: I examine every word you say. I try to sift the lies from the half-truths.

ROSEMARY/MIGUEL: I'm all about the truth.

ANI/BLANQUITA: It takes more than dinner.

ROSEMARY/MIGUEL: It takes days, then months.

ANI/BLANQUITA: And I learn to trust you.

ROSEMARY/MIGUEL: I learn to be faithful.

ANI/BLANQUITA: Not easy for a man with your disgusting reputation!

ROSEMARY/MIGUEL: I drive women crazy. Is that something I control? Talk to God, don't talk to me!

ANI/BLANQUITA: Well, tell those bitches they're all out of luck!

ROSEMARY/MIGUEL: Stop being so jealous, Blanquita!

ANI/BLANQUITA: My family doesn't trust you either.

ROSEMARY/MIGUEL: Because they're so white they think they're from Spain.

ANI/BLANQUITA: But your green eyes and dark Taino skin devastate me.

ROSEMARY/MIGUEL: And we marry.

ANI/BLANQUITA: In an old church.

ROSEMARY/MIGUEL: With an ageless, life-sized crucifix of wood.

ANI/BLANQUITA: Then. Slowly. Easily. With visions of angels in our heads.

ROSEMARY/MIGUEL: And in our dreams, night after night . . .

ANI/BLANQUITA: We make a child.

ROSEMARY/MIGUEL: We make a child.

ANI/BLANQUITA: We make a child.

ROSEMARY/MIGUEL: The child is beautiful, with long wild hair and dark eyes and she's the third, final, and most perfect part of this little world we've created. She saves us from each other, from the wild animals that stalk our imaginations. She's our purpose, our compass. Something in her that seems to keep us alert through all the morbid dangers of daily life . . . like a good-luck charm.

(Ani/Blanquita and Rosemary/Miguel turn to Mayannah.)

ANI/BLANQUITA: Are you hungry, mija?

(There's the sound of rain as it pelts the big windows.)

MAYANNAH: No.
ROSEMARY/MIGUEL: Why not?
MAYANNAH: Cuz.
ROSEMARY/MIGUEL: Oh, I know why . . .

(Rosemary/Miguel mimes the crucifixion and laughs.)

ANI/BLANQUITA: Don't tease her again, Miguel.
ROSEMARY/MIGUEL: When did I say anything?—
MAYANNAH: You're laughing.
ANI/BLANQUITA: She's sensitive.
ROSEMARY/MIGUEL: Ay Dios, when did I say a word?—
ANI/BLANQUITA: If she starts crying again . . .
ROSEMARY/MIGUEL: She's not going to cry. Are you, Mayannah?
MAYANNAH: No. Depends.
ROSEMARY/MIGUEL: You made a little mistake. There's not enough
    light in that stupid church. And, when you think about it, they
    don't have to make it look so real. So bloody. Sadistic Catholic
    bastards!

(Ani/Blanquita laughs, crosses herself.)

ANI/BLANQUITA: Ay Dios, Miguel, watch what you say in front of
    the child!
ROSEMARY/MIGUEL: Right, mi cielo?
MAYANNAH: Sí. Catholic bastards.
ANI/BLANQUITA: I hope you're pleased with yourself!
MAYANNAH: Do I have to eat?
ANI/BLANQUITA: Of course you have to eat. This is the last night
    we're going to eat together for three weeks.

MAYANNAH: Jesus killed my appetite.

ROSEMARY/MIGUEL: ¡Ven aquí!

ANI/BLANQUITA: You're going to spoil our last dinner . . .

ROSEMARY/MIGUEL: Pobrecita. ¡Que te vengas aquí, carajo!

(Mayannah approaches Rosemary/Miguel tentatively.)

MAYANNAH: Not funny, Papi.

ROSEMARY/MIGUEL: I know, my sweet angel of an angel, I know . . .

(Rosemary/Miguel and Mayannah hold each other a long moment.)

MAYANNAH: Okay, I'm hungry now.

ANI/BLANQUITA: How the hell do you do that?

ROSEMARY/MIGUEL: Now sit down now and stop being foolish, boba.

MAYANNAH: Yes, Papi.

(Mayannah sits. Ani/Blanquita serves food.)

ROSEMARY/MIGUEL: This lechón smells like heaven itself . . .

MAYANNAH: We shouldn't eat meat.

ROSEMARY/MIGUEL: Pity the poor vegetarian, I say!

(Ani/Blanquita pours rum and lights black candles.
Mayannah runs to the record player and turns it on, excited.
A bolero plays.)

ANI/BLANQUITA: What are you going to do while we're gone besides
miss us?

MAYANNAH: Book report.

ROSEMARY/MIGUEL: On?

MAYANNAH: Tigers!

ROSEMARY/MIGUEL: Ah!

MAYANNAH: I said it a million times!

ANI/BLANQUITA: You don't need to be sarcastic, young lady.

MAYANNAH: But he never remembers! Ugh!

ROSEMARY/MIGUEL: My memory. Worthless! Shoot me in the head, por Dios!

(Ani/Blanquita smiles at Rosemary/Miguel.)

ANI/BLANQUITA: I can't tell you how excited I am about this trip. We need this trip.

(Rosemary/Miguel and Ani/Blanquita hold each other and dance close. Rosemary/Miguel smiles at Mayannah.)

ROSEMARY/MIGUEL: Oye. We'll take pictures for you. We'll have many, many pictures of tigers for your book report.

MAYANNAH: It's not fair. Why can't you take me? I can help. I'm not a baby. The Jesus in church—scared me. His eyes did. It's bad luck if you see Jesus still alive. I read that in the stupid Bible! If you go without me, it's bad. I feel it. And you can't leave me with La Doña. She's a big, fat liar! Please? What if I never see you again? Mami, Papi, will you please take me to India with you to see the tigers?

(Rosemary/Miguel and Ani/Blanquita look at each other.)

ROSEMARY/MIGUEL: What do you think?

ANI/BLANQUITA: We made our plans.

ROSEMARY/MIGUEL: Can't we change our plans?

ANI/BLANQUITA: Can we change what's already done?

ROSEMARY/MIGUEL: She's been good.

ANI/BLANQUITA: Can we change what's meant to be?

ROSEMARY/MIGUEL: We can change whatever we want to change, Blanquita.

ANI/BLANQUITA: She's been so very good, that's true.

ROSEMARY/MIGUEL: She has been perfect.

MAYANNAH: Is that yes?

(Slightest beat.
 Rosemary/Miguel and Ani/Blanquita stop dancing.)

ROSEMARY/MIGUEL: Sí, mi cielo. The answer, tonight—is always—
was always—and will forever be always—

(Mayannah can barely believe it . . .)

MAYANNAH: . . . Yes!

*(Rosemary/Miguel and Ani/Blanquita sit at the table. Mayan-
nah hugs them both.)*

. . . yes, I'm going.

*(Mayannah looks around—at her resurrected parents, at the
world that's completely changed.)*

I'm going.

*(Mayannah pours herself a shot of rum, takes a sip, and
coughs. Ani/Blanquita and Rosemary/Miguel laugh at her and
begin to eat.*
 *The family eats together, lively, animated, laughing . . . As
the lights go down on them, the bolero gets louder, and police
sirens fill the air—then blackout.)*

END OF PLAY

Pablo and Andrew
at the
Altar of Words

·)⊹(·

PRODUCTION HISTORY

In November 2011 *Pablo and Andrew at the Altar of Words* premiered
as part of an evening of plays on the theme of same-sex marriage,
called "Standing on Ceremony: The Gay Marriage Plays," at the
Minetta Lane Playhouse in New York City. It was directed by
Stuart Ross. Sarah Zeitler was the set designer. Josh Starr was the
lighting designer. The cast was as follows:

PABLO	Mark Consuelos
ANDREW	Craig Bierko

A wedding chapel.

    Two men, Pablo and Andrew, face each other.
    An unseen Priest stands upstage of them.
    Pablo turns to the audience/congregation.

PABLO: So, we wrote our own vows and stuff.

ANDREW: Then we memorized them and they say a lot about the kind of love we want to express to each other.

PABLO: They say the things we never really say in this hugely titanic struggle it can sometimes be just to survive, day to day.

ANDREW: We went through how many drafts?

PABLO: Because we wanted to capture something that can't be caught.

ANDREW: To swear in front of these friends here today and our somewhat bewildered family members—yes, I mean you, Aunt Rosa—and to swear, also, before whatever great, loving, immense, fearless, life-loving force put this beautiful man on this beautiful Earth for me to admire and devour . . .

PABLO: God is great. God is good. ¡Viva Dios!

ANDREW: To swear to listen. To swear to protect. To swear to applaud. To swear to cultivate the right kinds of silence.

PABLO: To swear to criticize in the most constructive manner.

ANDREW: To swear patience despite the ever-accelerating kick-ass of time.

PABLO: To swear peace even when, inside our minds, a war may rage, a storm may destroy the simple order of our thoughts and our souls.

ANDREW: To swear to never skip a day, phone it in, or coast easily through the few God-given hours we were blessed to take home.

PABLO: To swear an honest love, unblemished with lies, words that carry the simple codes of desire and want, openly, unashamed, unafraid.

ANDREW: To swear to be a guardian of your health.

PABLO: To swear to be the armed guard of your trust, your secrets, your private joys.

ANDREW: To swear to be the landlord of the hidden places where you are most vulnerable, the dark corners where you go to cry . . . I promise to wait there with strength and an ample shoulder . . . and other bodily comforts should the need arise.

PABLO (To the congregation): He improvised that last part! (Laughs) To cage your dragons and teach them to behave.

ANDREW: To dream your dreams for you when they're too big for you to carry and kill the dark angels of your doubts and smooth the road ahead so you may walk into your sunshine and claim what's rightfully yours.

PABLO: To teach you to salsa dance.

ANDREW: To teach you to appreciate haggis.

PABLO: Ay, Dios, this is going to be harder than I ever imagined!

ANDREW: If marriage is about love, why would we want to reduce the amount of love in the world? If everything goes up—from the temperature of the clouds to the blood count of wars and the kids who die and die—then why can't the amount of love in this sad, old battlefield go up as well?

PABLO: I look at you and want to love you more. I see eyes that see me as I am. I speak words to a man who hears the anguish in my voice, knows where to find the laughter inside, can turn mere words into the music of compassion and pleasure.

ANDREW: I say good morning and he hears a Neruda love sonnet. I wake up looking like a creature from a Guillermo del Toro movie and this bright man, with an angel's eyes, sees somehow something that moves him to smile and not run away screaming to the nearest former boyfriend.

PABLO: Don't worry, dear, they've all been banished to a galaxy far, far away.

ANDREW: Then why are half of them in this church?

PABLO: Okay, now, back off!

(Andrew reaches into his pocket, takes out a ring.)

ANDREW: I have a ring in my hand, querido. It's made of the minerals of my absolute affection for you. It's inscribed with the tears of joy you make me cry when you don't even suspect you're doing a thing to me. It's worth more to me than all the world's supposed treasures because this simple circle fits around the infinite space that is the length and breadth of my adoration.

(Andrew slips the ring on Pablo's finger.
Pablo reaches into a pocket and pulls out a ring.)

PABLO: With this ring, precioso, I thee wed. I thee take. I thee embrace. I thee celebrate. I thee wash from head to toe. I thee articulate. I thee hold, through doubts and fevers and loss and the sweet, melancholy and eventual crumbling of our well-worn bodies.

(Pablo puts the ring on Andrew's finger. They hold hands.)

ANDREW: And from this day forth, I will lie with you . . .

PABLO: . . . in a bed of flames . . .

ANDREW: . . . in a bed of soft, lingering hope . . .

PABLO: . . . in a bed of moonlight . . .

ANDREW: . . . in a bed of ice cream and cake . . .

PABLO: . . . in a bed of spinning asteroids . . .

ANDREW: . . . in a bed of circus clowns . . .

PABLO: . . . in a bed of exclamation points!

ANDREW: And finally . . .

PABLO: . . . in the quiet, earthy, wormy, deep, secluded, cozy, encompassing, ravaging—and utterly nasty nasty juicy yummy little bed of our final rest.

ANDREW *(To the congregation)*: He improvised that last part.

(Andrew and Pablo kiss.
  Lights to black.)

END OF PLAY

Adoration

of the

Old Woman

·)┼(·

For Adena and Teo

•⟩✝⟨•

In September 2002 *Adoration of the Old Woman* received its world premiere at La Jolla Playhouse (Des McAnuff, Artistic Director; Terrence Dwyer, Managing Director). It was directed by Jo Bonney. Neil Patel was the set designer. Emilio Sosa was the costume designer. Christopher Akerlind was the lighting designer. Darron L. West was the sound designer. Diana Moser was the stage manager. The cast was as follows:

ADORACIÓN	Marisol Padilla Sanchez
DOÑA BELÉN	Ivonne Coll
VANESSA	Tamara Mello
ISMAEL	Gary Perez
CHEO	John Ortiz

CHARACTERS

ADORACIÓN, a sexy, beautiful spirit, twenties

DOÑA BELÉN, a fierce, indomitable country woman,
between one hundred and one hundred and fifty years old

VANESSA, an inner-city New Jersey girl, seventeen

ISMAEL, a large, powerfully built man, thirty

CHEO, an idealist, twenty-six

SETTING

Las Arenas, Puerto Rico.

TIME

Near future.

Act One

·)|(·

SCENE 1

Early morning, January 6.

    A one-bedroom, concrete house in rural, near-future Puerto Rico.

    A porch with a rocking chair. Living room. Bedroom.

    All brightly painted, adorned with religious artifacts, but run-down, some mold on the walls.

    A mattress set on a wooden palette, raised off the ground by bricks, is Belén's bed. An elaborately carved headboard decorated with santos, Madonnas, stuffed white birds, crosses, the hair of dead children.

    A machete leans against the wall.

    A door to the offstage bathroom.

    Two women lie in bed—ancient Doña Belén and young, beautiful Adoración.

ADORACIÓN: —It's true! Nobody's got an education in Las Arenas, but you don't need one when rumors are ripe and sweet.

BELÉN *(Praying)*: Mary, dear Mary—apocalyptic Mother of God!

ADORACIÓN: And the new ones are delicious! Rumors of war, independence, forests full of guerrilleros, caves full of machetes.

BELÉN *(Praying)*: Virgin womb, divine seed-carrier, blessed tit that suckled our Savior!

ADORACIÓN: Listen to me, old woman, you'll learn something.

BELÉN *(Praying)*: Holy nipples, full of grace—hard, sweet, may the thirsty tongue of Christ lick you day and night!

ADORACIÓN: Ay, slow down there, lady!

BELÉN *(Praying)*: Creative Mother of divine light, take away the darkness hovering over my bed!

ADORACIÓN *(Getting closer to Belén)*: If the people vote for independence and the gringos say no, will a war really come? God! There's no way the gringos will beat Puerto Rico this time! . . . There are too many soldiers, you know, buried below us. Patriots who died without firing a shot or raising a machete in anger. Their blood stains the clay and enriches the trees. This is the army of our liberation, all the proud dead.

(Belén pushes Adoración.)

BELÉN: Move over.

ADORACIÓN: You move over. Fat cow. Ugly fat cow ass.

(Adoración slaps Belén on the ass.)

BELÉN: If Christ Jesus can endure hours of torture on the Tree of Suffering, I can, too!

ADORACIÓN: Don't be so righteous! I've seen your fat ass swing from house to house like an aguacate tree in a hurricane, spreading your rumors and telling your lies.

BELÉN: I don't lie. You do. You can't breathe without lying. And you're a whore too!

ADORACIÓN *(Laughing)*: Is "whore" the best you can do?

BELÉN: Bitch!

ADORACIÓN *(Laughs)*: Oooooo stop.

BELÉN: Marriage-destroying, scheming, two-faced, dog-licking slut-bitch!

ADORACIÓN *(Laughing)*: Fine, all right.

BELÉN: You can go to Hell and burn in Hell and leave me alone.

ADORACIÓN: Ay, dear Doña Belén you don't know what you're talking about. I know about Hell. I've seen it. When I say "Hell" I know what I'm saying.

BELÉN: You've seen it, huh? Have you seen my cunt?

ADORACIÓN: You talk about Hell but you might as well be talking about Ponce or Mayaguez because you've never seen those places, you don't know them, and you don't know Hell.

BELÉN: Smell my cunt.

ADORACIÓN: I can't believe you talk about that horrible thing so much. Like it's something I even want to imagine.

BELÉN: You don't have to imagine it. I'll show it to you.

(Belén makes a face, imitating her cunt.)

ADORACIÓN: Just beautiful. Makes me wish I were a man, like our beloved Don Toli, with a long, hard tree between my legs.

BELÉN: My cunt looks like the opening to Hell. Now, shut up and let me sleep.

*(Belén closes her eyes and tries to sleep.
Adoración puts her arms around her.)*

ADORACIÓN: I'll tell you why we campesinos have so many rumors. When you don't have money, you have words. *Information* is what keeps a little barrio like this—so poor and isolated— feeling alive. But rumors go bad. They get mixed with lies and travel like a virus through the guts of the town, making everyone sick, and no bruja can cure it.

BELÉN: Is that what killed you? The rumors?

ADORACIÓN: Your ugly words did it, as if you didn't know!

BELÉN: Well, it should've been a knife, carajo! A sharp one!

ADORACIÓN: Ay, you have an ugly mind!

BELÉN: I wish I had opened your chest with Toli's machete. Yanked your heart out of this corrupted body—this dry, meatless rag. How any man could stick it into this smelly, little hole of yours—

ADORACIÓN: Stop it right now!—

BELÉN: This is *my* bed. Toli made this bed for *me*. I slept here. Loved here. Had seven miscarriages here. I do an old woman's lonely work and I collapse here every night. You don't tell me what to do in my bed!

ADORACIÓN: Yeah? Well, while you were at church, telling God your lies, your husband, your dear Don Toli and I were in this bed, fucking like dogs.

BELÉN *(Crying)*: . . . ay, no more, stop . . .

(Adoración laughs, stretches out luxuriously.)

ADORACIÓN: God gives us a body to use. A voice to scream it. Legs to encircle. Hips to bear the weight. All the while . . . you expand, you inflate, to fill the world with your joy. I was breakfast, lunch and dinner for that poor, hungry man . . .

(A knock at Belén's door. They look at each other, apprehensive. Belén gets out of bed and shuffles to the living room. Adoración waits and listens.
In the living room, Belén opens the door.
Vanessa is there, surrounded by suitcases. Vanessa is seventeen, dressed in dark urban clothes, heavy boots—completely wrong for the tropical sun—sunglasses, bandana, low-cut jeans.
Though we hear English, Belén is speaking Spanish, Vanessa is speaking English, and neither can understand the other.)

VANESSA: Great-grandmother?

BELÉN: Who the hell are you?

VANESSA: It's me Vanessa.

BELÉN *(Trying to be pleasant)*: Whatever you're selling, girl, tell K-Mart I don't want it.

VANESSA: Vanessa. My name. Vanessa. Va-ne-ssa!

BELÉN: Yes, yes, Va-ne-ssa, for the love of God!

VANESSA: Vanessa from Paterson—my mom wrote to you? My parents are *Florida and Enrique Aponte*?

BELÉN: Those names are vaguely familiar . . .

VANESSA *(Reading a scrap of paper)*: Are you Doña Belén Berdecia?

BELÉN: I am Doña Belén Berdecia Aleida.

VANESSA *(Showing Belén the paper)*: Are we in Las Arenas?

BELÉN *(Can't read)*: What's wrong with this idiot child?

VANESSA: Mami wrote you letters 'cause you have no *phone* . . .

(Vanessa takes out a cell phone, punches a number.)

BELÉN: If you're a Mormon you can take the warmed-over Jesus you bought at K-Mart and shove it up the ass of your gringo bosses.

VANESSA *(On the phone)*: Mami? Vanessa.

BELÉN *(Regarding the telephone)*: What the hell is that thing?

VANESSA *(On the phone)*: I'm standing right in front of her. She looks like she wants to hit me. And she's old. And her house is a shack. Here.

(Vanessa holds the phone out to Belén.)

BELÉN: Don't put that thing in my hand.

VANESSA: Tel-e-phone-i-o?

BELÉN: Ay, it's a *telephone*! Where the hell's the wire? God Almighty. The gringos have done away with civilization at last. They can talk to the air!

VANESSA *(Into the phone)*: The town that time forgot, yo!

(Belén takes the phone.)

BELÉN *(On the phone)*: What? . . . Yes . . . You're *Celia's* daughter? *My* Celia? Ay, my dear granddaughter! Ay, Florida, the last time I saw you, you had shit running down your leg and

I chased you half way to Jerusalem before you let me change your diaper! May God bless you and keep you in the glorious light of Jesus the Son . . . Yes . . . Yes.

(Vanessa finds three unopened letters from her parents on Belén's table.)

VANESSA: Yo lady! You're supposed to *read* your mail!

(Grabs the phone.)

This is horseshit, if you think this is good for me, you're outta your—*shut it, Mami*—I'm gonna find drugs, and do them, and shoplift, and jump an unemployed slacker Puerto Rican, have his bastard baby, and you're gonna look like the biggest asshole in the—

(Her mother hangs up.
  Vanessa turns the phone off.
  Belén looks at Vanessa, tears in her eyes.)

BELÉN: Look at you, bendito, so full of gentle sweetness and love, my dear great-granddaughter . . .

(Belén embraces Vanessa and covers her face in kisses. She makes the sign of the cross over Vanessa's face and chest.)

VANESSA *(Pulling away)*: Quit that shit.
BELÉN: I see my husband Toli in your eyes, God rest his soul, and Celia in those lips, God rest her soul, and the souls of my seven unborn babies, taken from this ungrateful shit-world too soon, swept from the floor of the world by God before I got a chance to mourn them—God rest their souls! Sit, sit, oh God you're too skinny, just a *rag*, I have some chocolate and cigarettes.
VANESSA *(To the universe)*: This is my tomb right here, right now.
BELÉN: I see the Puerto Rican in you, though you've done every-thing in your power to disguise it, those gringo clothes, vulgar

shoes—you don't smell like any woman I've ever smelled, yet you *are* Boricua. They can keep you prisoner a hundred years, the Boricua will always show. I see it as I see it in myself. It's the beautiful thing you hide from the world.

(Vanessa takes out a Spanish/English phrase book.
Bold in dialogue indicates characters have switched to a second language, which they speak with thick accents.)

VANESSA: **I. Am. Vanessa.**

BELÉN *(Shaking her head)*: Ay, it's a sin how they have corrupted your soul. You lost your humanity because you're looking out for number one. That's what they do up in Paterson.

VANESSA: Paterson! I live there!

BELÉN: They take our little flowers—the bloom and glory of His Imagination, the pride of our culture—and shit all over them.

VANESSA *(Reading from phrase book)*: **I am well. How are you?**

BELÉN: I'm fine, thank you, how are you?

VANESSA: **Do you have? A room for bathing?**

BELÉN: Do I have a what?

VANESSA: Jesus, it's not like they bothered to teach me Spanish! Oh, Mami's a blond now! She goes by Flo, nobody calls her Florida. She's being such a white bitch it's not even funny.

BELÉN: Don't you know a single word?

VANESSA: Don't you know a single word?

BELÉN: Ay, what have they done to your language?

VANESSA: **Bathroom?**

BELÉN: **Good morning, Teacher.**

VANESSA: Good morning, Teacher? . . . That's so good. Good morning, Teacher.

BELÉN: **Good morning, Teacher!**

VANESSA: Lookit, I'm gonna find el BATHROOM, before I URINATE on el floor-io?

(Vanessa squats, pantomiming going to the bathroom.)

BELÉN *(Shocked, pointing off)*: The bathroom's through there, child, don't be stupid!

(Vanessa crosses to Belén's bedroom on the way to the bathroom.
Adoración sees Vanessa.
Vanessa pauses in the bedroom, senses something—then exits to the offstage bathroom.
Belén "talks to" Vanessa's mother, Florida, as if she were there.)

Of course, I'll take your daughter in, she's blood after all. I know it's popular with the gringos to deny blood and let your family die in the streets covered in snow, even on Three Kings Day, but that's not how things are done down here!

VANESSA *(Off)*: Your bathroom is disgusting!

(Belén "talks to" Vanessa as if Vanessa were in the room.)

BELÉN: You're very angry, aren't you, child? The anger comes from having a hole in your body and I don't mean the little one between your legs. I mean the one in your heart. It's the hole normally filled by God, the saints and most of the popes. You tried to fill that hole with things. Shoes, lipstick—sex—yes, sex—because I have serious doubts about your virginity, girl. Those things don't fill the hole. They go in and fall forever, because the hole of God in the human body is infinite. It can't be filled with K-Mart. The body knows this and feels cheated. So there's anger. Storms and waterfalls of anger. You're consumed by it, little angel.

ISMAEL'S VOICE: Where's the queen of the house? The queen of my affections?

(Ismael enters. He is a large man, thirty, powerfully built, with fat, soft hands. He brings a chainsaw.)

BELÉN: Ay, Ismael, come in, my dear son—you brought it?

(Ismael holds up the chainsaw.)

ISMAEL: The exorcist of God.

BELÉN *(Excited, to Ismael)*: May the Heavenly Saints protect you from the violence of the Coming Apocalypse!

ISMAEL: Thank you and I hope you're right. The only blood I want to see on Judgment Day is the blood of animals and the Castro brothers.

BELÉN: Ah, but in the end, my beloved, animals, too, will enjoy the blissful reunion with the Heavenly Architect. As for the commies, fuck 'em . . .

ISMAEL *(Skeptical)*: Animals are going to Heaven?

BELÉN: Yes! All living things are going.

ISMAEL: Scorpions and tarantulas, too?

BELÉN: Well—maybe not exactly scorpions and tarantulas . . .

ISMAEL: What about the mosquitoes?

BELÉN *(Getting annoyed)*: Okay, no, the mosquitoes will be exempt from the Glorious Explosion of Peace, now that I think about it!

ISMAEL *(Teasing her)*: Cockroaches? Fleas? Centipedes? Maggots? Lice?

(Vanessa reenters, zipping her fly.)

BELÉN: Ismael! Meet Vanessa! My great-granddaughter from North America, Paterson. Inside that angry face and those barbaric clothes is a beautiful Boricua flower.

ISMAEL *(Holding out his hand)*: It's a pleasure to meet you. Welcome to our enchanted island. Pearl of the Caribbean. My name is Ismael.

VANESSA *(With no hope, to Ismael)*: Do you speak any English, please oh please?

(Ismael switches to a fluent, slightly accented English.)

ISMAEL: **I do, young lady.**

175

VANESSA: Thank God!

ISMAEL *(Good-natured laugh)*: Doña Belén's English is limited.

VANESSA: To, "Good morning, Teacher!"

BELÉN: Good morning, Teacher!

ISMAEL: Are you on vacation, Vanessa?

VANESSA: Vacation? Try total, degrading exile in some fucking third-world gulag!

ISMAEL *(Laughs)*: You speak English at the university level.

BELÉN *(To Ismael)*: Ay, isn't she beautiful? She'd make a challenging wife, Ismael.

ISMAEL *(Proud, to Vanessa)*: Do you know your great-grandmother is between a hundred and a hundred and fifty years old? Some say she was born the year of our liberation from Spain, 1898, a treasure of this barrio. But no one knows for sure.

BELÉN *(Impatient)*: And tell her about the bed! About the depth of my suffering. How the moon looks down on me and laughs!

ISMAEL *(Holds her)*: Bendito, poor, sainted Doña . . .

BELÉN: If I knew how to write, I'd send the pope a letter and he'd understand. Only you understand. May the Holy Spirit fold his wings around the armor of your heavy heart and burn away your sorrows.

ISMAEL *(To Vanessa)*: Her bed is haunted. Every night the ghost of Adoración Celia Lomar lies next to her. The ghost whispers in Doña's ear, telling her lies and pornography, making the old woman go crazy. No photos exist of her, but they say Adoración was the most beautiful girl in Las Arenas—don't tell la Doña I said that! She was poor, religious, her father beat her for being independent. They say she used to yell at the American foremen in the sugarcane fields, in English: "Why you no give them water? Why you no pay more money? Capitalist pricks!" . . . But despite all that, she was best known for being the mistress of Don Toli.

BELÉN: I was beautiful. I had a figure like a violin.

(As Belén tells this story, Ismael whispers a simultaneous English translation into Vanessa's ear.)

ISMAEL *(Sotto to Vanessa)*: **I had a figure like a violin . . .**

BELÉN: You could tell by my hips that I would bear a hundred powerful children. I couldn't read but I knew everything there was to know about men and women. About love itself. I had a sense of humor. I could sing. I could carry my weight in barrels of water and bundles of sugarcane. I could slaughter pigs. I could love all night. And men are so stupid, they have the very best, yet they're never satisfied. They sniff the air. "Ah, I smell some available pussy over there." How much more pussy does a man need, I ask you!

ISMAEL *(Translating to Vanessa)*: **How much more pussy does a man need, I ask you!**

VANESSA: A pertinent question!

BELÉN: Toli had a Caribbean queen. But it wasn't enough for him. He wanted the Mulatta Whore of Las Arenas. It was my destiny to love a man other women adored. I could have picked an ugly man, a monkey who smelled like piss. No. My man smelled like honey. Well, nobody takes what's mine! I had sixteen brothers and sisters and if I wanted a drink of water or a cup of rice I fought them all like a savage and I got what was mine—even with hookworms eating my guts!

ISMAEL *(Sotto to Vanessa)*: **. . . even with hookworms eating my guts.**

VANESSA: Whoa. Awesome.

(Belén impatiently pushes Vanessa and Ismael into her bedroom.)

ISMAEL *(Entering room, whispering to Vanessa)*: **Rumor is—Adoración died in childbirth. Having Toli's baby.**

VANESSA: Fuckin' nice.

*(In the bedroom, Ismael and Vanessa do not see Adoración.
Vanessa admires the beautiful bed.
Adoración's eyes are fixed on Vanessa.)*

ADORACIÓN: Oh my dear God . . .

ISMAEL: Doña killed half the chickens in the barrio trying to get rid of the ghost—nothing worked. Now she goes from house to house, looking for someone to cut the bed in half. She wants me to take the haunted half to the woods to burn it.

BELÉN *(Blessing the chainsaw)*: May God bless the sparky plugs and iron teeth of this holy chainsaw, amen.

ISMAEL: Amen.

(Ismael pulls the chord on the chainsaw. It sputters. He pulls repeatedly—nothing happens.)

I don't know what's wrong with it.

BELÉN: God, no. Not another night in hell!

ISMAEL: It was working this morning.

BELÉN: The whore's put a spell on it!

ISMAEL *(Checking the chainsaw)*: I don't get it, it's brand-new—

BELÉN *(To Ismael)*: Get out! Go! Take that piece of shit with you! Imbecile! Loser!

ADORACIÓN *(To Belén, regarding Vanessa)*: I know her eyes, Belén! . . .

BELÉN *(To Adoración)*: I swear by the mother that bore you, if I catch you looking at her, I'll rip your eyes out . . .

(To Ismael and Vanessa.)

What are you idiots looking at? Get out!

*(Belén tries to give Ismael a cocotaso.
    Ismael and Vanessa rush out of the room.
    Belén collapses on the bed.)*

VANESSA: What just happened?

ISMAEL: You stay long enough you'll learn the whole island's full of ghosts. And they all want a piece of you.

VANESSA: Oh, thank you, that's just what I needed to hear.

ISMAEL: Listen, este, you want someone to get you out of this? Maybe hit a few hot casinos in San Juan . . . ?

VANESSA: Hello? I'm seventeen?

ISMAEL: **My grandmother was seventeen when she gave birth to her fourth son—**

(Vanessa shoves Ismael and his chainsaw out to the porch.)

VANESSA: And you're older than my pops?

ISMAEL: **Good! It's settled! I'll come by tonight. I'm taking you to El Quince. Wear something sexy. I want every man in this town to piss his pants when they see us together!**

(Ismael exits.

Vanessa puts headphones on and walks around the house smashing bugs.)

SCENE 2

Gorgeous sunset. Streetlights, porch lights and the TV are on.
Coquís chirp. The windows and doors are closed, locked. The living room floor is clean.
Adoración lurks nearby.
Belén, on the sofa, watches TV.
Vanessa sits next to Belén. She's changed her clothes and looks less foreign. She's on her cell phone, leaving a message for her mother.

VANESSA: I helped the old lady make rice and beans. I washed her floor. I took a walk and saw nothing but dead baby cows on the ground, broken pickups in all the yards, massive vegetation smothering the world. Oh, but, I found a mango tree and I stuffed my face, yummmm! Then I watched a tarantula TAKE ONE WHOLE HOUR to fuckin' cross the street. At sundown, the old lady makes me come inside like I'm gonna get kidnapped or something and locks all the doors and windows like it's Rikers Island! I'm stuck watching *Bonanza* and *Gomer Pyle* reruns! So I went in the bathroom and masturbated for an hour, okay? That's right, Ma, the word "masturbated" is now on your voice mail—twice! You should try it sometime! Day one and I have exhausted my imagination on this friggin' place. It's a prison and I want *out*. Call me, Flo, tell me you've made arrangements for my liberation!

(Vanessa turns off the phone.
    From a distance, in the dark, a cuatro plays—a sweet, old jíbaro melody.)
    Kevin Betances, twenty-six, a.k.a. Cheo, appears wearing a gold, tinfoil crown, a long tattered purple robe and a bad, fake beard.
    He sings a folk ballad celebrating Three Kings Day.
    Hearing the music, Belén grabs the machete and rushes out to the porch. She calls to Vanessa who stares dully at the TV.)

BELÉN: Ay, listen to that, child! I bet they don't play music like that in Paterson!

(Sings and dances along.)

Yes, Cheo, you remember the sacred days.

(Cheo finishes his song.
    Belén reaches into her bosom and takes out a dollar, which she puts in the tin cup Cheo has strapped to his belt.)

CHEO: My angel, my inspiration, the First Lady of Puerto Rico!

(Belén kisses Cheo.)

BELÉN: My son, why are you alone? I seem to remember there were three Wise Men . . .
CHEO: I went from house to house, I couldn't find two people to be the other kings. They'd rather be watching *Bonanza* reruns.

BELÉN: We live in the dark ages, my sweet son.
CHEO: Not for long. I promise you.

(Shows the dollar she gave him.)

This will help.
BELÉN: Just be careful. I hear the FBI is everywhere. They put you in jail and experiment on your genitals.

(Drawn by the voices, bored with TV, Vanessa comes out to the porch, sees Cheo in his absurd costume, and laughs.)

VANESSA: So who knew it was Halloween already?
CHEO *(To Belén)*: I'm sorry, I didn't know you had company . . .
BELÉN: My great-granddaughter from Paterson, God help me.

(Cheo takes off the fake beard and crown. He's handsome with intense, melancholy eyes.
Vanessa likes how good-looking Cheo is.)

VANESSA: Oh.
CHEO *(Smiles, to Vanessa)*: So? Didn't you enjoy the music? Where's your dollar for the cause?
BELÉN *(To Vanessa)*: This is Cheo. He and his followers are doing important work for the island. And the animals. I hear fewer coquís every night and Cheo's going to change that.
CHEO *(To Vanessa)*: It's the sewage they pour in our lagoons, instead of the beaches, where the tourists go. Doña Belén won't listen, but I think it was pollution that caused her seven miscarriages.
BELÉN: Atheist! Gringo!
CHEO: Surely you want to help us out, miss.
BELÉN: Vanessa doesn't speak the language. A Puerto Rican without language is a ghost.

(When Cheo switches to English there's NO CHANGE in accent.)

CHEO *(To Vanessa)*: You don't speak a single word?

VANESSA: I've had a long day, Pancho. Long. Day.

CHEO: The name's Cheo. And what's wrong with you? Why don't you speak Spanish?

BELÉN *(Impatient)*: Ay, tell her about the coquí! The tragedy!

CHEO *(To Vanessa)*: That chirping you hear? That's the coquí. It's a little green tree frog about the size of a—

BELÉN *(Delighted)*: Tell her about the Elulutherodoodlecacalo.

CHEO *(Trying not to laugh)*: The coquí is the official symbol of Puerto Rico. We have sixteen species. The most common of which is the Eleutherodactylus coquí—

BELÉN *(Delighted)*: A-hah! That one! I love that one! Say it again!

CHEO: Eleutherodactylus!

BELÉN: It's like music!

CHEO: On this side of the island we have mostly Eleutherodactylus antillencis. They're all dying out, every species. In the last twenty years, we've tragically lost the golden coquí, Eneida's coquí and coquí palmeado.

VANESSA *(Could care less)*: That's tragic all right. What's up with the rags?

CHEO: Don't you know what I'm wearing? *(To Belén)* I bet she's never even heard of Three Kings Day!

BELÉN *(To Cheo)*: But I bet she can tell you where to buy marijuana.

VANESSA *(Excited, to Cheo)*: Did she say marijuana?

CHEO *(Trying to stay patient)*: Do you even know what this island's going through right now? The election we're about to have?

VANESSA: I know I heard marijuana!

BELÉN: She'd make a challenging wife, Cheo . . .
      (Looking at Vanessa's ass) . . . but we'd have to work very hard on that ass of hers.

CHEO *(Looking)*: Yeah. Way bony.

BELÉN *(Pantomiming a big ass)*: After a month of my cooking, bendito, that ass is going to be as round and ripe and juicy as a—

CHEO *(Laughs)*: . . . as a mango, no, a papaya, no, like a, like a . . .

VANESSA: Motherfucker, stop talking about my ass, and tell me what's fucking going on around here!

CHEO: Girl, it's election time in Puerto Rico! Which makes Puerto Rico even crazier than normal! Want to hear the awesome speech I gave in Arecibo last week?

VANESSA: Not especially.

CHEO: I'd be happy to oblige!

(Cheo jumps on the porch and speaks as if before a crowd.)

"Puerto Rico must vote for freedom and independence! It must turn it's back on the travesty of Commonwealth! Listen to me, my comrades, my people, my blood! If Puerto Rico votes to become a state of the United States, forget it! We will be shitting on our past, dishonoring the dead, lobotomizing the future and performing in an absurdest tragedy worthy of Jean Genet!"

VANESSA: That is so boring, it numbs the mind.

CHEO *(Laughs)*: Why thank you. Want to hear it again?

VANESSA: Glad to help out. And no.

CHEO: Half this barrio thinks I'm crazy, the other half ignores me but the sad truth is, in five hundred years, we've been a free people for only a week and a day. And that has to change.

(To Belén.)

Right? Independence?

BELÉN: Long live the free, democratic Republic of Puerto Rico!

CHEO *(To Vanessa)*: See? My people know! They know in their instincts!

BELÉN *(To Vanessa)*: He's going to be governor some day, you watch!

CHEO: Governor? President!

BELÉN: Maybe even dictator! If we're lucky!

CHEO *(To Vanessa)*: Our cause is just. And it's dedicated to the memory of Pedro Albizu Campos. Do you know who he was? I didn't think so. He's Puerto Rico's George Washington. Do you know what the U.S. did to that genius? I didn't think so. They stuck him like a dog in a prison and roasted him alive with radiation—which they injected directly into his body. A human experiment until the day he died, paid for by your tax dollars. You can read all about him on usgetthefuckoutofpuertorico.com.

ISMAEL'S VOICE: **All that about Albizu Campos is such total bullshit.**

(Ismael appears out of the darkness, dressed nicely.)

CHEO: Oh! The pussy man is here!

BELÉN *(Dreading a fight between the men; to Cheo)*: Cheo, why don't you play something sweet by Los Reyes de la Plena? Or Trio Boricua?

CHEO *(To Ismael)*: You just don't want to believe what your precious USA is capable of—

ISMAEL: **That rumor was never proven, Kevin. Radiation!**

VANESSA *(To Cheo)*: Kevin? I thought it was Cheo.

CHEO *(To Vanessa)*: Kevin Alejandro Betances, at your service. No relation to the great freedom fighter, but you probably never heard of him either.

ISMAEL: **But he calls himself Cheo because "Che" was already taken by that Argentine faggot.**

CHEO *(To Ismael)*: Don't you have to bomb Vieques or something?

BELÉN: No, no—you are both my angels—no fighting—

ISMAEL: **I came to see if Vanessa wants to go to El Quince. We could get some beers, listen to the Stones, shoot pool and totally chill . . .**

CHEO *(To Vanessa, laughing)*: Lucky Vanessa. About to experience the joy of sex with Tio Taco . . .

BELÉN *(Alarmed)*: You were like brothers, and it breaks my heart—

ISMAEL *(Angry, to Cheo)*: **You need to take your doomed, dead, nationalistic bullshit and get lost, Kevin. It's sad the way you hold on to this shit. It's over. Statehood's going to win. Time to forget these romantic ideas of a "nation" called Puerto Rico.**

CHEO: He can't stand it. The thought of Puerto Rico being free.

ISMAEL: **The U.S. gave him everything and he hates it. But ask him what the life expectancy was before the U.S. came in. Thirty-five years. Now it's seventy.**

VANESSA: That's a good point . . .

CHEO: Seventy years of grinding poverty, disease, exploitation, political limbo—oh, sign me up.

ISMAEL *(To Cheo)*: **Come on, bro, do you really think, after all this time, the U.S. can just pull out of Puerto Rico?**

CHEO: Why not?

ISMAEL: **We need statehood to save us from ourselves. René Marqués was right, we're docile, politically apathetic, childish and naive . . .**

(Anticipating Cheo's response.)

After five hundred years of colonial rule—?

CHEO *(Overlapping)*: After five hundred years of colonial rule? What the hell do you expect?

ISMAEL: **I give up, you win.** *(To Vanessa)* **Let's go.**

CHEO: No, no, no—you gotta tell me, Izzy—I want to know how the U.S. can tolerate a state full of people who don't want to fucking be a state.

ISMAEL: **I don't know, bro, ask Alaska, ask Hawaii.**

CHEO: Ask Quebec.

ISMAEL: **Will you shut up and let me take Vanessa to El Quince?!**

CHEO *(Imitating Ismael)*: Here, Uncle Sam, here are my balls. I don't know how to use them. Maybe you could teach me, sir.

(Playful, to Vanessa.)

C'mon, give me a point for that . . .

(Vanessa laughs.)

ISMAEL: **And what's going to happen the day *after* independence? Well, first, everyone on the island will lose their U.S. citizenship. No more U.S. passports! Then anyone with half an education will book a flight to Ohio. Then we're going to realize that we don't have free access to the U.S. markets anymore. Then our**

186

pretty new currency with the pretty little face of Pedro Albizu Campos will collapse.

CHEO: Then the Cubans are going to come in—

ISMAEL: **Then the Cubans are going to come in—**

CHEO: And then we're going to starve to death.

ISMAEL: **And then we're going to starve to death—that's right!**

CHEO: The old "Cuba" argument! The old "starve to death!" Compai, it's a tropical fucking island. Shit *grows* here.

ISMAEL: **You know there's not enough land or skill in Puerto Rico to feed everyone.**

CHEO: The Tainos did it. With no technology. And we could do it too if every decent acre of land hadn't been stolen by the empire in the name of King Sugar.

ISMAEL *(Laughs)*: **"Empire"? "King Sugar"? Wow. Just wow.**

CHEO: And you know for a fact the independence parties are asking the United States for a long transition, with enough foreign aid to keep us afloat—

ISMAEL: **Why the fuck should the U.S. give us a penny after we reject the gift of statehood?**

CHEO: Payback for all the labor and resources and wealth their corporations stole?

ISMAEL: **You believe in fairy tales, bro. I believe in a bunch of new members of the House of Representatives and two senators— that's the real prize. Right now, Cheo, any pig-faced red-neck senator from Mississippi can decide what life in Puerto Rico should be like. I'd love to see a Puerto Rican senator changing life in Mississippi.**

VANESSA *(To Ismael)*: Slam dunk!

ISMAEL: Eso!

CHEO *(Dismissive)*: All he's getting is a ton of new federal and state regulations and taxes and a complete loss of dignity.

ISMAEL: **So full of shit. We'd have much more dignity as a state. We earned this. We paid a blood tax in all the U.S. wars. My grandfather paid the ultimate price in France. Two uncles in Vietnam. Statehood is a gift paid for by our dead. Statehood is a moral imperative.**

CHEO: Statehood is the murder of a nation.

ISMAEL: *I shit on that argument!* You have a utopia in your head—happy little jíbaros in their shacks of straw, wearing pavas, on their mules, free to dance their coplas and décimas, to pray to Las Siete Potencias and make babies. This island nearly starved in the thirties and forties. Look at the pictures. Malaria, hookworm, malnutrition. It's in the *eyes*. In those doomed jíbaro eyes you love to romanticize.

CHEO: You know why he believes in statehood?

ISMAEL: Now? We're happy. We've got our malls, Toyotas, cable, internet. It's called progress, you commie, Fidel-loving fuck!

CHEO: He sells real estate. He thinks the property values will skyrocket if we go statehood. But he loves to forget that most North Americans don't want us in their precious country—

ISMAEL: *Bitch! I'm going to fucking break your neck!*—

BELÉN: My grandfather was killed the day of the gringo invasion!

(Cheo and Ismael go silent as they look at Belén, who tries not to cry.)

My family watched the soldiers walk through Arecibo, laughing, like it was a joke, a picnic. We put up almost no resistance—except for abuelo. He fired his old pistol, wounded himself in the foot, and they turned their rifles on him and decorated his valor with their bullets.

(Cheo and Ismael go to comfort Belén.)

ISMAEL *(To Cheo)*: **You made her cry.**

CHEO *(To Ismael)*: You made her cry.

VANESSA: You assholes made her cry!

(Vanessa strokes Belén's hair until Belén smiles.)

You okay, sweetie?

BELÉN *(To Vanessa)*: Okay.

(Cheo and Ismael go silent, their anger and indignation tempo-rarily spent as they hold Belén.

Vanessa looks at the two passionate, young men fighting for her attention. Maybe being in Puerto Rico won't be so bad . . .)

VANESSA: Okay. It's close, boys. Very close. *(To Ismael)* I hope you shoot pool good as you talk, bro.

ISMAEL: **I'm your man! Tonight and every night of the week!**

(Vanessa and Ismael disappear into the darkness.

Cheo, comforting Belén, watches Vanessa and Ismael dis-appear, then walks Belén into the house.)

SCENE 3

*Later. The sofa in the living room has been made up for Vanessa to
sleep on. The TV is on.*

Cheo is asleep in the rocking chair, on the porch.

*Adoración has been in bed with Belén for hours, kissing her,
stroking her long hair.*

Belén stares at the ceiling, rigid with anger and insomnia.

ADORACIÓN: . . . No, Don Toli wasn't the strongest man in Las
Arenas. But you never measure a man's true strength by the
amount of suffering he can take or the amount of cane he can
cut in a day or how many shots of rum it takes to make him
smile after a day of hard labor. When I took water to the men
in the fields, or filled my fiambrera with hot asopao, I treated
each man like he was a king. I knew work was scarce and
soon the tiempo muerto would come and the guajana would
cover the fields and there would be no work for nine months
and much suffering. Yes, women whispered that I was a whore

because I went to those fields to refresh the men with water and soup, even though I had no husband, or novio, and a girl my age was never allowed alone in those fields with all those men. But I didn't care about the rumors and dirty words! Those men were heroes in my eyes, each one, not mules like the foremen thought. Each man was a soldier fighting against the starvation that always seemed only a day or two away. It shocked me that every woman in Las Arenas wasn't out there with me. The nerve of those bitches calling me whore! . . . The first time I gave Don Toli his cold water, I *knew*. How a man can work under the hot sun, bent like an animal, and still have the willpower for sexy thoughts is beyond me. He took my water. And, later, he took the rest of me without lifting a finger. Sometimes you come face to face with your definition of manhood. Not your mother's, not your religion's, not your barrio's. Yours. And I did.

(Belén slaps Adoración across the face.

Adoración feels no pain and doesn't react.

Belén slaps her again and again—and again there's no reaction.

In frustration, Belén gets out of bed, goes to the sofa, collapses.

Vanessa and Ismael approach the porch.)

ISMAEL *(Laughs, regarding Cheo)*: **Your guard dog's waiting. Don't you feel safer?**

(Cheo wakes up, regards them darkly.)

CHEO: Doña couldn't sleep because of the ghost. I told her I'd stick around.

ISMAEL *(Knowing why he's really there)*: **Uh-huh. Don't you have to bomb the people who bomb Vieques?**

CHEO: Ours is a nonviolent movement, Izzy, like . . .

ISMAEL: **. . . like Gandhi and César Chávez and blahddy blah blah.** *(To Vanessa)* **Call me if you need anything. I'm the house with** the American flag on the second floor. The one with fifty-one stars. I could take you to old San Juan, Luquillo Beach, Ponce, El Yunque—

CHEO: The next couple of weeks could be a bad time to travel.

ISMAEL *(To Cheo)*: **Was I directing this statement to you?**

> *(To Vanessa)* **You tell me, I'll take you, okay? I got friends that will keep us safe. And tell him to keep his hands to himself. Bye.**

VANESSA: You should fuckin' talk!

(Ismael exits.
Cheo and Vanessa look at each other, awkward.
Vanessa looks at the night sky, listens to the coquís.)

You don't see Milky Ways like that in Paterson.

CHEO: While you're in Puerto Rico, you should take a real good look around. Before it's too late. And don't do it with Izzy—he only knows what the tourists know. Promise me you'll do that?

VANESSA: Why's it so important to you that I do that?

CHEO: Because all this is gonna be gone some day. Little neighborhoods like Las Arenas, their little plots of land, full of chickens and pigs, this semi-independent way of life. It's all disappearing, like the coquí. Getting buried—as the highways get closer. Even the stories told by old women like Doña Belén, the stories that hold these barrios together and connect the past with the present. All that's dying.

VANESSA *(Looking around)*: Looks to me like it ain't changed since like the early Jurassic Period.

(Cheo looks at her, wondering how much he can confide.)

CHEO: There was a place I used to swim in, when I was a kid. On the beach, outside Arecibo, beautiful little bay called La Posa. It was my spot. Diving off the rocks. Time would stop for us. Black kids, white kids, we were one color—the color of little

ADORATION OF THE OLD WOMAN

fish. And the ocean was our home. The sun was our clock. Nobody was hungry in that water. Nobody was ignorant. I used to think—it must've been like this for the Tainos. Perfect, pure, endless. One day I walked there. And there's a fence. La Posa was bought by a U.S. hotel chain and the thing that was mine—and all us kids—was out of reach. For the fucking rich tourists.

(Vanessa studies Cheo's face a long moment.)

VANESSA: Yeah, well that would suck.
CHEO: I hated that fence, man. Made my hands and feet bloody trying to do kung fu on it. Begged Doña Belén to hit it with a curse. But La Posa died. When I stopped breaking my hands, I went home to think, and I realized the only way out of this was nonviolent political action. That's all I've thought about since. Now I'm a month away from finding out if I wasted my life.
VANESSA: Izzy was saying, every time there's an election your side only gets like three percent of the vote.
CHEO: I think I know my people, Vanessa.
VANESSA: I'm just saying.
CHEO: My people are so damn restless, so ready for a new concept of home, we're on the verge of exploding! Something's going to be born next month. The question is *what.*

(Vanessa doesn't answer right away. She studies him again.)

VANESSA: But you don't seem that Puerto Rican to me.

(Cheo thinks about this.)

CHEO: My parents sent me to a prep school in New Hampshire.
VANESSA: Aha! I knew he was a gringo!
CHEO: It gets worse. I went to NYU. Then grad school in Boston.
VANESSA: Mighty whitey!

CHEO: I even got a job offer with the State Department.

VANESSA: Now you must die.

CHEO: But I just couldn't take it. The day after I got my master's I was on a plane to San Juan. Immediately I hooked up with my old friends. Night after night, we talked about change, *real* change, not a theory of change, and *now*, not waiting for the next generation to save our ass, like our parents waited. You know, I got a bicycle and rode from one end of the island to the other? Took me a fucking year. And my ass hurt the whole time! Fuck, it still hurts!

(Vanessa laughs.)

VANESSA: You ever take a night off from the Crusade?

CHEO: Why?

VANESSA: 'Cause I think what we gotta do is climb that fence, say fuck you to the tourists, and swim naked in La Posa tomorrow night. Tell me that ain't revolutionary, bitch.

CHEO *(Surprised, pleased)*: That sounds cool but I—I have to be at a rally in Ponce tomorrow night—

VANESSA: Day after?

CHEO: I'd like to but I need to spend every minute this month organizing to get out the vote.

VANESSA: So there's no way to get together and break a few rules around here?

CHEO: Why don't you work with me? On the campaign.

VANESSA: But I'm suggesting something fun.

CHEO: I lead a small nonviolent cell, twelve of us share a house in Arecibo. We're the Grito de Lares Movement. Twelve little people trying to do the work of a hundred. North-central Puerto Rico is my precinct and I could sure use your help.

VANESSA: But I don't even speak Español!

CHEO: It doesn't have to be a lot. You could stuff envelopes, hand out pamphlets in the plaza—

VANESSA: No, stop, that sounds too fucking hot. Just hearing the word pamphlet makes me want to take my clothes off.

CHEO: Come on, you're a Puerto Rican woman, this is your country calling!

VANESSA: My country is Jersey, yo!

CHEO: ¡Pero todavía lleva la mancha de plátano!

VANESSA: Like I even know what that means!

CHEO: You're scared. I'm scared, too. All us independent fighters are. I mean, you don't know how many death threats we get every week. People out there actually want to decapitate us!

VANESSA: Damn, bro, you could sell ice to the polar bears with a rap like that!

CHEO: No, no, come on, you'd be on a tropical island, having a fucking adventure.

VANESSA: It's just—shit, okay, you're gonna be mad.

CHEO: What?

VANESSA: Well, how do you really know you're right about this thing? What if Izzy's right and you get freedom and you starve to death? Or the Cubans invade? And everyone's gotta wear long beards and smoke cigars and shit? Isn't that—really possible?

(Cheo takes a breath. This isn't going to work. He leans over and kisses Vanessa softly on the cheek, surprising her.)

CHEO: You know what? It's good Doña Belén has family with her, she's lonely.

VANESSA: Was that as random as it felt? . . .

CHEO: But I have a shitload of work to do and no time. I'm sorry you won't be with me as we make a new country. I just hope you find yourself connected to this place, because it's *in* you, Vanessa. It might even be the best part of you.

VANESSA: Okay, now you're pissed at me for being honest.

CHEO: I'm sorry. This isn't a game. Or a TV show. Or a costume drama we natives are putting on for the tourists.

VANESSA: And now you're insulting my fucking intelligence.

CHEO: I'll see you again when we're free. I'll see you when we're free.

(Cheo exits.

Vanessa watches Cheo leave. Disappointed, Vanessa goes into the house, sees Belén asleep on the sofa. Watches her. Adjusts her blanket.

In her sleep, Belén "talks to" Don Toli.)

BELÉN *(In her sleep)*: I don't want to get pregnant anymore, Toli.

(As Toli) What are you talking about, Belén, shut up.

(As herself) It's not that I don't want to make love!

(As Toli) It's a sin to talk to your husband about making love! Stop it!

(As herself) But when I'm pregnant, I'm not *me* anymore. I'm God's servant. Delivering another soul to the world. I can't eat, and everything makes me vomit and it feels like a war in my womb. Why does God put the seed in my belly and make my body fight it? What acid, what poison, do I shower on the fetus, suffocating her and stopping her heart? Why did God give me seven of them? Why did God erase them? Ay, no more, Toli, no! Let's silence our passion and be like brother and sister from now on. I'll cook and honor and care for you. I'll doctor your wounds and sing away your nightmares. I'll be your wall and your sanctuary. God will never find fault with our love, Toli. He'll know its purity is as clean as any marriage, like Mary and Joseph, even if we never touch each other again.

(As Toli) You talk like a witch. I'm a man, Belén, and I must have what a man must have. I won't have the men of Las Arenas think less of me. This house will have a child. Bless me, Belén.

(As herself) May God bless you, Toli.

(As Toli) Again.

(As herself) May God in His Infinite Compassion embrace you, Toli, and bless your home with children, children, children.

(Vanessa goes to the bedroom and sits on the bed.

Adoración sits with her.

Vanessa lies on the bed.
Adoración lies with her.
Vanessa can sense her. She fights her impulse to flee in terror.)

VANESSA: Adoración?
ADORACIÓN: Welcome to Las Arenas, angel.

(Vanessa sits up, gasps.
Terrified, Vanessa gets out of bed. She grabs Toli's machete—and brings it down violently on the headboard of the bed.
Blackout.)

Act Two

·)|(·

Scene 1

A month later.

Belén's bed has been cut in half. The two halves of the bed sit side by side.

The house is clean and decorated with Puerto Rican flags. Banners proclaim: "¡Vota por Independencia!" "¡Nacionalismo Sí!" "¡Annexación No!" Etc.

In the dark, Cheo's voice:

CHEO'S VOICE *(Singing)*:
>¡Despierta, borinqueño,
>que han dado la señal!
>¡Despierta de ese sueño
>que es hora de luchar!

(The quiet barrio has changed. In the distance we hear fire-crackers, campaign music from rival camps, political speeches delivered on loudspeakers on passing cars, shouts, cheers, helicopters, fighter jets, the rumble of heavy vehicles.

The sounds rise in volume, hit a peak, then die down.
Belén lies on one of the halves of the bed, very ill.
Adoración lurks nearby.

Vanessa sits at Belén's side, spoon-feeding asopao to Belén.
Vanessa hums the song Cheo sang when they met and eats
slices of mango with great relish.

Vanessa is subtly changed. Her clothes and hair resemble
Adoración. She has an easier, sexier manner. She's put on a few
pounds and wears no makeup.)

BELÉN *(Very ill, labored)*: There was a time I was considered the most beautiful girl in the world. I could perform miracles with my beauty. Cure diseases. Inspire poets. I had those poems here somewhere, but I think I lost them. Shit! Scientists from around the world came to Las Arenas to study me, the actual reincarnation of Helen of Troy, may God protect that heathen bitch.

VANESSA *(Halting, heavily accented)*: **My Little-Grandma. Many, many beautifuls . . .**

BELÉN *(To Vanessa)*: And arrogant! No man alive could get near me. From the time I was twelve, I shunned them all, put them in their place, old men, sexy men, powerful men . . .

VANESSA: **Soup good? Hungry more soup?**

BELÉN: Only one man was unmoved by my magic. He was quiet and modest, my reputation and charm meant nothing to him. And I fell for that sneaky motherfucker so fast, it wasn't even funny.

(Vanessa can see there's no way she can make Belén eat.)

VANESSA: **Water?**
BELÉN: Rum.
VANESSA: **Water.**

(Vanessa goes off to get Belén water.
Adoración approaches Belén.)

200

ADORACIÓN: Why do you hold on to this miserable life, huh? Look at you. You're a ghoul. You were never that beautiful to begin with! I was. Even your parents said so! And I'm still beautiful. My skin doesn't drag on the ground. My hair is full of wind and sunshine. Put your hand between my legs. I didn't dry up!

BELÉN *(Weak)*: Do you see how Vanessa takes care of me? . . .

ADORACIÓN: People say the dead walk the earth because we have unfinished business. But sometimes I think it's the *living* who keep us here with *their* unfinished work. Fights they should have had. Revelations that came too late. Lovers they can't let go. What do you want to learn from me, you old whore, that you don't already know? Why do you keep me here? Huh? You won't die, you won't let me go, and you won't let me talk to Vanessa . . .

BELÉN *(Weak)*: When I die, Vanessa will say such beautiful things at my funeral . . .

ADORACIÓN *(Fierce)*: After I died, Don Toli left your bed that night and walked to my grave, crying the whole way!

BELÉN *(Violent)*: Liar! He *danced* on your grave! He danced a samba!

ADORACIÓN *(Grabbing Belén roughly)*: I gave you this fever. The bloody diarrhea. I'm in your guts like a worm. Slowly melting each of your bones. But it's not happening fast enough.

(Adoración kisses Belén full on the mouth and gropes her.

Belén nearly suffocates in the violent kiss. She struggles and pushes Adoración away.

Belén stumbles to the offstage bathroom and vomits.

Alarmed by the noise, Vanessa comes back on, holding a glass of water. She can hear Belén in the bathroom, throwing up.

Cheo enters and approaches the porch. Exhausted, unshaven, he's been working nonstop all month and hasn't slept in three days.

Vanessa's back is to him as she listens, concerned, outside Belén's bathroom.)

CHEO: Vanessa?

(Vanessa turns around to see him, pleased, relieved, as he is. Time has only intensified the attraction.)

VANESSA: I'm good, thanks for asking. Yes it's been a lonely month, thanks for calling, thanks for stopping by—

CHEO: Be nice. I haven't slept in three days.

VANESSA: You look it. So you finished all the great work?

CHEO: All I know is it's the last day. When the polls close at nine, that's it. It's literally history.

VANESSA: Came by to say hi to the girl in the haunted house? Who's been hearing voices at night. And crying! I had to cut the bed in half it got so bad!

CHEO: You're brave to take on a Puerto Rican ghost.

VANESSA: Well, it didn't help. She's stalking me. I keep seeing a weird woman in my dreams. Whispering to me all the time . . . So what are you doing here?

CHEO: I came by to take Doña Belén to vote. And to say hi to Vanessa, who looks like she's quite at home, ghosts and all.

VANESSA: Yes and I learned how to make sofrito too. And oh, that mofongo, man? That pernil? I could OD on that fucking shit.

CHEO: You even pronounced it right.

VANESSA: So are you sticking around this time or do you gotta liberate the Virgin Islands, too? I hear Guam is looking to start some trouble.

CHEO: Tonight I'm going to the safe house in Arecibo to watch the returns on TV. Would you like to go to Arecibo with me?

VANESSA: Actually, yeah I would, but great-grandma's sick, so I'm gonna stay.

CHEO: What's wrong with her?

VANESSA: Fever, the shits, but she tells me not to worry.

CHEO: You understand her?

VANESSA: Another month and I'll be speaking at the university level.

CHEO: Impress me.

VANESSA *(Haltingly)*: **The sky is blue. The beans are cold.**

CHEO: Complete sentences . . .

VANESSA: **The little pink ducks are homosexual.**

CHEO *(Laughs)*: Very useful phrase.

(Vanessa looks him over, smiles.)

VANESSA: Ay, this tropical heat! On every inch there's something alive, something eating, or fighting, or fucking. It's like a feast and a funeral all at the same time. Making me have some real strange yearnings.

(Sexy smile) God gives us a body to use, Cheo. A voice to scream it. Legs to encircle. Hips to bear the weight.

CHEO: That's an interesting thing to say . . .

(A fighter jet streaks across the sky over them.)

VANESSA: Wild, huh? Fighter jets. Those riots in Ponce, man, I couldn't believe those.

CHEO: You heard about that?

VANESSA: I was there! Just after it happened. I went to San Juan too. Oh, and I met these students from Río Piedras who said, like, the U.S. Navy's gonna surround the island if independence wins tonight.

CHEO: My friends in the New Nationalist Party heard the U.S. Congress is going to annul the vote if it's not statehood.

VANESSA: And there's some Puerto Rican army—living in the rain forest . . . ?

CHEO: A guerilla army in El Yunque, planning an assault on San Juan if we become the fifty-first state. They say they've got caves filled with machetes. And they're gonna turn El Yunque into the next Sierra Maestra.

(A moment as she looks at him.)

VANESSA: A couple of days ago, I caught a car to Arecibo and I found La Posa. I saw the fence. And I tried to picture this skinny little angry boy doing kung fu on it, beating his hands all bloody.

CHEO: And his feet.

(Beat.)

VANESSA: I was kinda hoping I'd run into you out there . . .
CHEO: When things settle down, you and I are going to steal some time, and I'm going to take you to some amazing places. I swear you're not going to believe your eyes.

(Vanessa walks away from Cheo.)

VANESSA: But I'm going home next week. I'm leaving Puerto Rico.
CHEO: Just when you're starting to feel at home here?
VANESSA: Cheo, my Papi's in trouble again. He's got some fucking stupid problems and he's been in and out of prison and rehab since he was eighteen.
CHEO: But the next few months, after there's independence . . .
VANESSA: Look, man, my father is still a child. He got high and punched me in the mouth 'cause I was wearing shorts he didn't like for fucksakes! "I don't like how it makes your ass look! Like a whore's ass." And all I could do was laugh! "Bitch, stop staring at my ass all day!" Another smack! More blood!
   (Trying not to cry) All that blood between my teeth. Tasting like salt seawater. The same blood I spit in his ugly face. It's why my mother sent me out here. To fucking chill and protect me from his rampaging. But she's a useless child, too, and she can't handle him alone and she needs me to come back like yesterday.

(Cheo goes to her, holds her tightly, then kisses her, mouths lingering gently together.)

CHEO: This month I shook a thousand hands, gave out flags, drank Don Q with old-timers with stories of Don Pedro. But sometimes all I wanted was to hear you mangle the Spanish language. And to try your burnt tostones.
VANESSA *(Holding him)*: I bet you wanted my tostones.

(She kisses him, longer, more.
  Belén shuffles into the living room.)

BELÉN: Sweet angels. When's the wedding?

(Vanessa and Cheo pull apart.)

CHEO: How do you feel?
BELÉN: Who cares? I'm only one person. A speck of sand on God's
  beach. A teardrop in His eye.
CHEO *(Going to her)*: I care about you.
BELÉN: No, no, bigger things are happening today. Are we going to
  kick those gringos off our island or what?
CHEO: We're going to try.

(Vanessa grabs Belén's sweater and Bible)

BELÉN: All our brothers and sisters. Migrating north to get rich,
  leaving us to starve and wait. Marriages, deaths, births, bap-
  tisms—all happened in Philadelphia and Newark and Lower
  East Side. Not on the soil that conceived them. Why couldn't
  they put their sweat and sacrifice into *this* land? Why did
  they ruin their minds in a place that compared them to cockroaches? So bright, young, hopeful. Kidnapped by advertising,
  imprisoned by snow, buried alive in bricks and subways.
CHEO *(To Belén)*: Are you ready to do this?
BELÉN: I may be dying, but that won't stop me from fighting for my
  country against General Electric, Westinghouse and the Pres-
  byterian Church!
CHEO: Let's go and vote, my angel. Let's make history.

(Belén clasps her hands together.)

BELÉN: Be our liberator tonight. And you will see the most grateful
  nation the world has ever known. Amen.

(Cheo, Vanessa and Belén leave.
  Firecrackers, horns honking, shouts.)

SCENE 2

That night.

Vanessa is riveted to the TV. The light and noise of the TV fill the room.

Sicker than ever, Belén sits on the sofa next to Vanessa. Belén's stomach hurts.

BELÉN: Ay, that damn bitch did it. She put worms in my insides . . .

VANESSA *(Torn between the TV and Belén)*: Do you want something to eat? **Food, eat?**

BELÉN: Vanessa, I knew you'd be good to me because you're my Celia's granddaughter. We could be separated by mountains and generations yet the blood we have is strong!

(Belén starts to cry.)

VANESSA: Hey, hey, no.

BELÉN *(To Vanessa, weak, afraid)*: Please, Vanessa, don't let me die. Don't let Adoración take my life, Vanessa, please don't let her!

VANESSA *(To Belén)*: If you could just *slow down* a little—

BELÉN *(To Vanessa)*: None of my organs work. My eyes see shadows and nothing else. I've started to shit myself.

VANESSA: **Slower, slower . . .**

BELÉN: But I don't want to let this go. I don't want to face God. I don't want him to judge my sins!

VANESSA: **Doctor? Please? Doctor?**

BELÉN: Fuck doctors! They waste your time and steal your hope and help themselves to everything in the bank!

VANESSA: No doctors, check.

BELÉN: Do you know how many Hail Marys I've said in my life? How many rosary beads I've worn down to nothing? All for what?

(The sound of gunshots outside the house.)

What the hell's that?

(Before she can answer, a sound on the TV gets their attention.)

VANESSA *(Watching TV)*: Oh shit, here it comes. **Look! The news!**

BELÉN *(Trying to focus on the TV)*: All my life, elections were shown in Spanish! Why does this one have to be in English?

VANESSA *(Responding to the TV)*: **Little-Grandma,** you see what happened? **The street—people sing—dance.** Wild! Tanks. Battleships.

BELÉN: Did we win? Is Cheo president?

(Vanessa and Belén watch the TV in silence, then . . .)

VANESSA *(Indicating the TV)*: Oh my God. Oh fuck! No!

BELÉN *(Looking at the TV)*: Who is that ugly little man?

VANESSA: **That's the President of the United States.**

BELÉN: What the hell's he doing?

VANESSA: Celebrating, 'cause his country just got a little bigger . . . Fifty-two percent of the people of Puerto Rico went for statehood. **Independence—got—three percent.**

BELÉN *(Looking at the TV)*: We lost?

VANESSA: **Killed.**

BELÉN *(Sinking in)*: What? We lost?

VANESSA: The polls are closed. Yes. It's official. Look. There's the new American flag. With fifty-one stars.

(Belén clasps her hands.)

BELÉN: Ay! Endure, endure, little island.

(Vanessa turns off the TV and grabs her cell phone. She calls Cheo.
Belén prays.)

Take your peace where you can find it. Remember yourself. Go inside yourself. Under the soil. To the bones of our warriors. To the old songs and poems. We are not slaves, dear God. We are not slaves. Ay, poor Cheo!

VANESSA: You know where he is? **Where? Cheo?**

BELÉN: That poor boy, that poor son of Puerto Rico.

VANESSA: I've been trying his cell—

BELÉN *(Points to cupboard)*: Get me something to drink.

(Mimes.)

Drink.

VANESSA: **Sleeping. Please be sleeping.**

BELÉN *(Fierce)*: I said DRINK and I mean NOW and I mean RUM!

VANESSA *(Almost laughs)*: At your service, ma'am.

(Vanessa gets Belén rum and two shot glasses. They take shots.)

BELÉN *(Stronger)*: I will not, I will not, I will *not* be a North American.

(Gunshots. Shouts. Loud cars.)

VANESSA: They're going crazy out there.

(Belén crosses to the door.)

BELÉN: Ill-mannered, poorly raised, snot-nosed—
VANESSA: **Little-Grandma**, what're you—?

> *(Belén opens the door and limps out to the porch.*
> *Vanessa follows.)*

BELÉN *(Shouting to people offstage)*: What's wrong with all of you idiots? Don't you know what you've given away? Tonight you should be home! With your children! Thinking about the future! What kind of Puerto Rico have we become? What does it mean to be the fifty-first state of the United States?

> *(Gunshots subside. Cars drive away.*
> *A total silence we haven't heard before.)*

VANESSA: There's something weird out here.
BELÉN *(Crossing herself)*: The coquís have stopped singing . . .

> *(Belén and Vanessa listen to the strange silence and involun-*
> *tarily draw closer together.)*

Scene 3

Just before sunrise.
  Belén lies on the sofa, the bottle of rum in her hand.
  Vanessa sits on the porch, asleep on the rocking chair.
  Cheo appears. He's exhausted, a little drunk, animated by anger and self-pity. He holds a half-empty bottle of rum.

CHEO: Congratulations, America! You're on a roll, baby!

(Vanessa awakens, looks at him.)

VANESSA: Thank God you're alive . . .

(Vanessa goes to him, embraces him.
  Cheo pulls away, looks at her.)

CHEO: Why do you even want to be with me? Why should anyone give a fuck what I have to say? I wasn't educated here. I never had a job here. Look at my clothes, man. I'm a walking colony! "My people." What a fucking joke. You know how many fucking times I've said "my people" in my life? I never got the dirt of Puerto Rico on my *shoes*. The air of this island swept through me, I never breathed it in. I swear on my mother's eyes, I'm right at the point where a bullet to the head looks pretty good—

VANESSA: Stop talking like that, c'mon.

CHEO: All of us in the safe house. This family created around an idea. A principle. People who left marriages, sacrificed families. Ay, the hearts we broke. Last night *we* were broken. You could hear each spine snap. Couldn't even look at each other. Being Puerto Ricans we cried a lot. Some of us good atheists even said it was God's will.

VANESSA: Come to bed, you need the sleep . . .

CHEO: They have another star on their flag! Fifty used to be their magic number. So round. So clean. So North American. But now it's *past* fifty—the magic barrier is broken. How many little stars will they take after this? When will they stop? Until they have all the light? Until they own the sky?

(Vanessa takes Cheo's bottle of rum.)

VANESSA: All I'm saying, when the noise dies down, a little time passes, maybe it's gonna be clear this was the best thing that could have happened . . .

CHEO *(Not listening)*: We had a chance for something real. Something that could free all the energy we've had locked up for five hundred years. To never again ask permission of the superstate to wipe our own ass. I swear, if there was a war tomorrow—and who knows, that's all I'm saying. I say—take my body. Take the whole thing, the legs, the balls: it's yours: I give it up to the cause now.

VANESSA: No cause is worth your balls!

CHEO: Grito's been my home all these years. But the New Nationalist Party wants me in their leadership. Some of them came to the house tonight . . .

VANESSA: Who are they?

ISMAEL'S VOICE: The New Nationalists advocate violent military resistance to the United States.

VANESSA *(Quietly, to Cheo)*: So you're telling me what?

ISMAEL'S VOICE: What he's telling you is illegal.

(Ismael enters, a little drunk, wearing pro-statehood buttons and little American flags.)

CHEO: Izzy, you picked the wrong goddamn time—

ISMAEL: It's a great time. A great night to party! A great night for the United States and the cause of freedom and the stock market and land values and blahddy blah blah!

VANESSA: For real, Ismael, you gotta disappear right now.

ISMAEL *(To Cheo)*: Bendito. Reality is a little too hard to deal with, huh, Cheo? The time to dream childish dreams is over, friend. Se 'cabó!

CHEO: This vote tonight does not represent the will of the Puerto Rican—

ISMAEL: Maybe not *your* Puerto Ricans, but the *sane* Puerto Ricans—

CHEO: Confusing ballots, polling mistakes, uncounted votes, people being turned away . . .

ISMAEL: The UN Committee on Decolonization supervised the vote, coño!

CHEO: Like they're not in bed with the U.S.

ISMAEL: It's really tough when history with a capital H passes you by. Yet you cling to that rusty old idea that once made sense to you, once kept you alive, gave you hope and kept your *cock* hard!

(Cheo lunges at Ismael.
Ismael is swift, strong and a full-out fight erupts.
Belén comes out with a heavy saucepan and beats both men with it until they stop fighting.)

BELÉN: This is what they want! This is what they want! We can just kill ourselves to make them happy!

(There's blood on Cheo's face and Ismael's hands. Cheo lies on the ground motionless.)

ISMAEL *(To Vanessa)*: He's got nothing and he's going nowhere. He doesn't know how people laugh at him. Do you know what my future's going to be like? The doors that will open for me? Yeah, some people think I'm a joke. Ismael, the pussy man. The money man. Tío Taco. Mr. Coconut. Brown on the outside. White on the inside. The list goes on forever! And I know you think so, too. But I'm a *serious* man, Vanessa. And I want you with me in this serious and incredible time.

(Ismael leaves.
    Belén and Vanessa walk Cheo into the house.
    They lay Cheo down on the sofa.
    Vanessa lies next to Cheo. They hold each other.
    Belén gets a wet rag and gives it to Vanessa.
    Vanessa cleans away Cheo's blood.
    Lying together on the sofa, Cheo and Vanessa kiss each other passionately.
    Belén leaves the living room and goes out to the porch.
    Cheo and Vanessa begin to make love as the lights go to black.)

Scene 4

Lights come up. A few days later.
Belén lies on her half-bed, sleeping.
Adoración lies on the other half-bed.
Cheo and Vanessa in the living room, getting dressed.

VANESSA: You're outta your mind, mister. I said no and no is no.

CHEO: You can't—cielo—you can't say no—

VANESSA: Think I can, think I did.

CHEO: But it's just a meeting.

VANESSA: Oh really. Then why're people talking about bringing weapons to this "just a meeting"?

CHEO: Because the police have weapons.

VANESSA: The police have weapons because people are rioting.

CHEO: Half the riots are police riots. They do the damage, shoot at people, *we're* the ones taking the bad press.

VANESSA: There's a curfew—

CHEO: Uh-huh, a curfew. Martial law. Summary arrests. Detention without trial. Political executions on the street in the name of law and order. A great first week as the fifty-first state!

VANESSA: Well, I don't support this. Those people who keep calling, I don't trust them.

CHEO: But everyone from Grito and Sangre Libre will be there. The Nationalists are electing officers. I've been nominated for a leadership position. What am I going to tell them? I can't be part of my people's history because I'm in bed with my fucking girlfriend?

VANESSA: I know, in some universal female part of my gut, this is wrong for you. The militant way is not the way of the man I've been in bed with for a week. Who makes love better than anyone else. Am I right?

CHEO: Well, right.

VANESSA: Except this is not a culture that listens to its women, is my acute observation. Maybe you should put that in your constitution, huh?

CHEO: I'll make a note of it.

VANESSA: Thank you. And then what you should do is say no to these people and start your own group—

CHEO (Getting frustrated): Look, the Nationalists want all the independence parties to merge. Then. To go into hiding in El Yunque. And be part of the guerilla army.

VANESSA: And you're good with all this?

CHEO: I've been thinking about it, yeah.

VANESSA: Why are you thinking of giving up on the nonviolence that was so important to you?

CHEO: Because we tried it and, oh my God, it didn't seem to work too good!

VANESSA: So they throw a free election at you and you throw back a bomb?

CHEO: How could that election be free? With their fucking warships parked outside San Juan? Their guns aimed at us as we vote? When people think about that, and all the other shit the yanquis pulled, they're going to be mad enough to fight back.

VANESSA: And that's you, huh? Mad enough to fight back?

CHEO: This land's never spilled blood in a war for its own liberation. That might have to change. And very soon.

(Beat.)

VANESSA: Okay. I'm going with you.

CHEO: No. Not even an option—

VANESSA: Because you know it's dangerous—

CHEO: I'm sorry. There's no way they'll accept you!

VANESSA: They won't accept me? Then you make them fucking accept me.

CHEO: But these fucking death threats are real.

VANESSA: Then you're not friggin' going, bro!

CHEO: I'm sorry, Vanessa. I'll call as soon as it's over . . . Take care of Doña Belén.

(Cheo goes to kiss Vanessa, she pushes him away.)

VANESSA: Fucking be careful.

(Cheo leaves the house.
Vanessa watches him disappear.
Belén awakens, talks to herself.)

BELÉN *(As herself)*: The doctor said *eat*, Toli.

(Vanessa enters Belén's bedroom.
Adoración watches Vanessa.)

(As Toli) For the sake of God and the goddamn nails in the feet of Christ, I don't want to eat, Belén. The cancer owns my stomach!

VANESSA: **Little-Grandma?**

BELÉN *(As herself)*: Eat, Toli.

(As Toli) You're a deep, horrible woman, Belén, letting me die like this. To pretend to everyone you care about me. You always have my dinner ready. My clothes are always clean. You only want to get back at me for loving Adoración.

VANESSA: **Cheo. And me. Fighting.**

BELÉN *(As herself)*: Eat, Toli.

(As Toli) God alive! I'm the man you shared life with for fifty-four years! What could I do? You wouldn't touch me anymore—after all the miscarriages—you sinned first by denying me—you drove me to that girl, *you* did—you. Belén, precious, just say you forgive me one time and it's over. So I can die in peace.

(As herself) Eat, Toli.

(As Toli) It was decades ago, you cow! What are you holding on to? I'll be dead in a few days. It takes nothing away from you and I gain my soul.

(Long beat.)

You ugly, arrogant cunt! I shit on your eyes, Belén! I shit in your mouth!

(As herself) Eat, Toli.

*(Vanessa gets into bed with Belén, holds her.
Adoración whispers in Vanessa's ear.)*

ADORACIÓN: She never forgave Don Toli, Vanessa. She let him die in the worst way to die, so alone . . .

*(Vanessa sees Adoración for the first time and freezes.
Vanessa gets out of bed, pulling Belén along with her.)*

SCENE 5

Next night. Vanessa is on the porch with her cell phone.
  Belén lies on the sofa.
  Adoración lurks nearby.

VANESSA: Cheo. It's me again. I thought you'd call after the meeting.
  A day ago! Don't know if you're in jail or what. Belén's in bad
  shape. I dragged her out of bed. She's on the sofa away from
  the ghost.

(Whispers.)

I *saw* her. The ghost girl. I'm highly freaked. But I wanna talk
  to her. God, I'm losing my mind! Call immediately. I will put
  aside my outrage the second I hear your voice.

(Vanessa turns off the phone.
  Ismael approaches.)

ISMAEL: Vanessa?

(Vanessa turns, regards him with contempt.)

VANESSA: I'll break your face for what you did.
ISMAEL: I think you need to turn on your television.
VANESSA: Why?

(Ismael goes into Belén's house, turns on the TV.
A voice on the TV reads off names.
Vanessa watches in silence.)

ISMAEL: They say there was an FBI informant among the New
Nationalists. When the leaders from all the independence parties showed up, soldiers surrounded the house. There were
negotiations, a standoff. Then the shooting. They're calling it
"Massacre in Arecibo."

(Indicating the TV.)

To discourage any more uprisings, they're showing the names
of the dead. To prove they mean business.
VANESSA *(After a few moments)*: . . . Kevin Alejandro Betances . . .
ISMAEL: I thought he was wasting his time, pushing us into a civil
war. But I never wanted this. We grew up side by side, you
know. We used to swim in La Posa together.

(Beat. Vanessa is too numb to move or speak.)

I'll stay or go, whatever you want.
VANESSA *(Barely audible)*: Go, Izzy.
ISMAEL *(After a beat)*: God Almighty. What are we doing?

(Ismael leaves.
Vanessa, alone, watches TV.)

Scene 6

Three days later. Afternoon.
Belén, dressed in black, enters supported by Ismael wearing a black suit.

BELÉN: In the past. No matter how bad things got. Puerto Ricans were allowed to die in privacy. I've never seen armed police at a funeral before, Ismael, and television cameras.

ISMAEL: The police are there to keep the peace.

BELÉN: The same motherfuckers who shot him?—

ISMAEL: Nobody knows who shot who.

BELÉN: It's a sin to bring a rifle to a funeral! Says so somewhere in Genesis.

ISMAEL *(Has said it before)*: When they buried the other independence leaders, there was violence. I think the gringos—

BELÉN: The gringos have finished this island, Ismael! They took away a saint of a boy and they will take more and more of

220

them until all that's left to sleep with our women are the robots and zombies and degenerates and collaborators!

ISMAEL *(Admiring her grit)*: Seems like you're feeling better.

BELÉN: Something's been awakened here. I don't like how it feels anymore. The way people look at you now.

ISMAEL: We can't go back to being asleep.

BELÉN: This is an *island*, Ismael. A sweet island. It floats on the ocean like a cloud. It's made for loving and dreaming, and spending time with God and when death happened there was never this kind of rage.

ISMAEL: That was a long time ago, before we were born.

BELÉN: You're an imbecile but I still love you like a son.

ISMAEL *(Teasing her)*: You're much too kind, Doña Belén.

(Vanessa enters. She wears black. She crosses to Ismael.)

VANESSA: Thanks for walking her home, Izzy.

ISMAEL: I didn't want to say this at the funeral, there was enough tension, but friends from Las Arenas, who grew up with Kevin—I mean Cheo—we're thinking of holding a vigil for him, here, in two weeks. Completely nonviolent, nonpartisan, just a remembrance of the man. And I hope you can be there, too. And Doña Belén of course . . . And when it's over, I promise I'll do everything to make sure the actions of the police and FBI are investigated. Hear me? Then we'll see how good this gringo justice really is.

VANESSA *(Appreciatively)*: Maybe I'll say a few words at the vigil.

ISMAEL *(To Belén, regarding Vanessa)*: Boricua flower.

VANESSA: But I want to do it in Spanish, so you'll have to help me with the translation.

ISMAEL: Of course. If you need anything else, I'm the house with the Puerto Rican flag on the second floor.

(Ismael goes to Belén, kisses her.)

BELÉN: May the Everlasting Love of Christ be in the food you eat, the water that bathes you and in the eyes and words of everyone who loves you. Amen.

ISMAEL: Sleep in peace.

(Ismael leaves the house.
Belén watches Vanessa a moment.)

BELÉN *(Mimes drinking)*: Water?

VANESSA: **Rum.**

BELÉN: Now you're talking.

(Belén gets a bottle of rum.)

Toli and I used to make this shit at home. I don't have the energy to make it anymore. But I buy it by the bathtub-full.

(Belén hands Vanessa a full shot glass.
Vanessa downs it.
Vanessa's Spanish, though vastly improved, is still accented and halting.)

VANESSA: **More. Please.**

(Belén gives Vanessa another.)

BELÉN: **Good morning, Teacher.**

VANESSA: **Good morning, Little-Grandma.**

BELÉN: How are you, angel?

VANESSA: **Sad today.**

BELÉN: I know you loved him. I was so happy to see the two of you together.

VANESSA: **I think. My heart. Is killing me with pain. No eyes Cheo, no ears—no touch him. He is never.**

BELÉN: Only his body is gone, dear. Only. His Body. Is gone.

222

VANESSA: The body. It was. His hands, his kissings. His body was mine. Now it is the earth. All lost, he dead. All nothing, he dead. All dead, he dead. I wish God be dead! . . .

BELÉN: No my love, don't say that.

VANESSA: Yes! God is to crucify me. God is to hurt me. To make His skyhome . . .

BELÉN: Heaven.

VANESSA: He make Heaven happy for God. But hurt girl who is loving Cheo. It's all full of shit!

BELÉN: Full of shit? Who taught you to say full of shit?

VANESSA (Almost smiles): Cheo teach me. Shit, cunt, bitch, asshole, whore, pimp, pussy, dick, tits, blowjob, I shit on God, I shit on your mother, I shit on the president, I—

BELÉN: Okay, you can stop now, I didn't know Cheo was such a good teacher.

VANESSA: I was almost laughing. Cheo's, how you say it? Hole, earth.

BELÉN: Grave.

VANESSA: Cheo's grave. At the end, at the far end—

BELÉN: At the edge.

VANESSA: Cheo's grave at the edge of the cemetery. The fence. The other side, the little—

BELÉN: The little farm.

VANESSA: The little farm. The cow and the horses. To the fence. To watch Cheo, to be cover in dirt.

BELÉN: Being buried.

VANESSA: A cow and two horses go—

BELÉN: Went.

VANESSA: *Went* to the fence to watch Cheo being buried. Silent, and they is to is—big eyes! Their big eyes went watching us being buried Cheo.

BELÉN: They knew. They looked sympathetically at us, dear angel, and they came to say good-bye. I wonder if animals feel pity for us when they see us bury our children. If I were an animal or an angel I'd feel sorry for the pathetic death of men and women. Of all the animals in the world we're the only ones who don't know how to let go.

VANESSA: You were so beautiful today. God, I watched you during that funeral and I swear I could feel the earth spinning under me. I learned about birth and death and war and power by studying the lines on your face.

BELÉN: We old women know how to do funerals. I'm going to make us some food.

VANESSA: **I'm not hungry.**

BELÉN: You're going to eat this. I can make you eat.

VANESSA: **Okay, but I can make the food. You sick. You rest.**

BELÉN: I don't feel sick today. I want to cook for you and take care of you. May the Infinite Love of . . . oh, Christ, I'm too tired to come up with a good fucking blessing right now.

(Vanessa's cell phone rings.
Belén kisses Vanessa, then goes to the offstage kitchen.)

VANESSA *(On phone)*: Hi Mami . . . It was this morning . . . Fine but I'm more tired than I can explain. How's Papi? . . . Tell him hi, okay? And I love him. And I want him to be well, I really do . . . I'm going to stay. I'm not going back to Paterson and all the madness. I'm going to apply to the University of Puerto Rico at Rio Piedras. Soon as they reopen it and investigate the killings . . . I know it's dangerous! Don't make me curse you on the day I buried my boyfriend, okay? . . . Then come down here and get me, Ma! See this place for yourself! You know, you tell stories and play the music and get all weepy, but you're never here! And your Spanish is atrocious! So come here, stay here a little, and then we'll talk. Got it, Florida?

(She turns off the phone. She walks to Belén's half-bed and collapses.
Adoración gets into the half-bed with Vanessa.
Belén watches Vanessa lie in bed. Belén decides to let her stay. Belén goes out to the porch, lights up a cigarette, looks up at the stars, thinks.)

ADORACIÓN *(To Vanessa)*: The old lady, she lied to you. Yes, I slept with Don Toli and everyone in Las Arenas knew—including Doña Belén. But no one dared say a word. Then I got pregnant. And that changed everything. Don Toli stopped wanting me—completely. I was so desperate, one day I went to church to look for him. He was there—next to Belén. She looked at my growing belly, her mouth opened for one word—*whore*. Over and over—in front of God, Mary, the entire town. Soon I was known as the Mulatta Whore of Las Arenas. When Don Toli started saying it, too—the words were like knives right into my body! My baby was born. And the dirty words of Las Arenas killed me. The day I was buried, Don Toli came to my house and my mother gave him my baby. And he took my baby to Belén and said, "This is *our* baby now. Celia is *our* baby." Belén said yes. And took her in. And never told you that your grandmother Celia was my baby.

    (In English) **Vanessa—you my baby.**

(Vanessa looks at her, understanding but not being able to reply.)

Ay! It was what the old witch wanted more than anything. To make life. To see it coming out from between her legs. Complete, breathing. Hearing it laugh. Its little fingers scrambling up to touch her. She never had that. All her stillborn hopes are buried under a Ceiba tree in Las Arenas. Each branch of the tree is another dead hope. My one baby—my girl—walked away from all that death. To think, to pray—and maybe, somehow, if there's justice, to remember the passage from my body into the humid air. To remember the liquid I surrounded her with. The loving thunder of *my* heart. The salt seawater of *my* blood. I told you to live and you did . . .

(Adoración kisses Vanessa, who kisses and holds her.
    Vanessa gets out of bed.
    Adoración gets out of bed.

Vanessa goes to the porch, to Belén, sitting on the rocking chair.
Belén doesn't have to look at Vanessa to know what happened.)

VANESSA: **Is she my great-grandmother?**

(Belén starts to cry, a cry she can't control, a cry that seems to break her body in half.
Adoración watches.
Vanessa goes to Belén and holds her.)

Little-Grandma . . . it's okay . . .

(Belén wipes her eyes, and looks at Adoración.)

BELÉN: I'm the last of my kind, Vanessa. There's nobody like me in the whole world. What I carry in my skin. What I know of life. What I remember of this island. But I'm as fertile as a stone. I have nothing to pass on but a haunted bed, a couple of poems they wrote about me, but I don't know where they are. Shit! I wanted so much to see my mother in your smile. To hear my sisters on your tongue.

(Belén looks at Adoración. Her words are as much for Adoración as they are for Vanessa.)

Oh, my dear. Now I think I know the pain I made old Toli feel when I didn't forgive him for his infidelity. The pain I made your great-grandmother feel. The worst pain—the pain of extinction . . .

ADORACIÓN: Yes, Belén, yes.

(Adoración starts to leave the house.
Belén gets up from her chair. Faces Adoración.)

226

BELÉN: Adoración Celia Lomar!

(Adoración stops and looks at Belén.)

I am sorry I took your daughter and killed you with my words.
That was unkind of me.
ADORACIÓN: Ay, Belén . . .

(Adoración approaches Belén.)

BELÉN: Tell Toli that I'm sorry and that I understand something
I didn't understand before. I understand why he loved you.

(Adoración embraces Belén.
     The old adversaries hold each other.)

ADORACIÓN: Would you like to tell him yourself?
BELÉN: Is he near?
ADORACIÓN: Just beyond those trees. Too shy to come closer. Come
with me and see.

(Belén thinks about the implications. Looks around at the
world she's known for over a century.)

BELÉN: It's not mine anymore, this old island.
ADORACIÓN: Nor mine. Are you ready?

(Belén nods yes and goes to Vanessa, who's been watching this
scene with some awe and sadness.
     Belén embraces her.)

BELÉN: I'm going with my old friend now.
VANESSA: **Are you sure?**
BELÉN: I'm between a hundred and a hundred and fifty years old.
I think it's time.

VANESSA: **I'll miss you so much, Little-Grandma.**
BELÉN: Is that the best you can do? Have I taught you nothing?

(Vanessa touches Belén's ancient face and tries not to cry.)

VANESSA: **May you find a wild Heaven full of love. And a God that'll plant a joyous garden in your wounded heart, dear, adored Doña Belén. And peaceful stars. And a whole bunch of little angels that'll like do stuff for you all the time.**
BELÉN: Okay. That's enough.

(They kiss and Belén goes back to Adoración.
The women embrace and leave the house together. And disappear into the forest in silence.
Vanessa is alone now. The house is hers.
Vanessa goes into the house. Goes into the bedroom. Looks at the two half-beds. And gets an idea.
Lights change. It becomes night.
Vanessa calls out to the universe.)

VANESSA *(Imitating Belén)*: Kevin Alejandro Betances!

(Vanessa gets into bed and waits.
Nothing happens.
Vanessa pushes the two halves of the bed together.
Cheo appears. He looks at Vanessa, unsure.
Vanessa looks at him, smiles and taps the side of the bed next to her.
Cheo's melancholy smile. He gets into bed with her.
Lights begin to go down.
The young lovers hold each other.
Vanessa and Cheo fall asleep together in Belén's magic bed as the sound of coquís begins—and fills the stage.
Blackout.)

END OF PLAY

University of Southern California School of Theatre Commencement Speech

DELIVERED IN 2010

Congratulations, we're all colleagues now.

Having been perpetual students of an art form that can't be fully learned because all the stories haven't been told yet, we are now able practitioners.

Not only that, we're partisans in a great struggle that may seem holy to some and crazy to others, but is wildly quixotic even at the best of times.

We're all veterans of hope, sergeants and captains of an idealism and courage that seem anachronistic and beautifully, dolefully, painfully antique.

Because what we do, what we are trained to do, is to keep an ancient and sullied and disrespected and much maligned and amazing tradition alive.

231

We together keep the spoken word from going silent, spectacle from disappearing in the ones and zeros of forgetfulness, great life-and-death themes from dying of malnutrition, enormous characters and souls from the purgatory of indifference and ignorance.

Together we keep the the house of Atreus from foreclosure and the Skriker from extinction and Kent and Salem from dying of cancer and Pozzo from getting too lucky.

We are apostles of language, dreamers in blank verse, aristocrats of sight gags, archaeologists of gesture and dance and sword battles and mask-wearing and mythic games of tragic and comic consequences.

We bring Falstaff to the party and hope he doesn't get too drunk and pinch too many butts even as we enter through the back door and try to deliver dreamworlds to the wary and the postmodern and the unsuspecting.

We traffic in awe and metaphors and are impatient with the ordinary and expected.

We fight the inertia of silence and talk too loudly in polite locations and there is no Ritalin for us.

We don't succumb to psychoanalysis and the voodoo of easy answers.

We thrive on complexity and ask that our monsters truly terrify us, that our lovers truly slay us with their passion, that our magicians truly make something out of nothing and hand it to us with smoke and a rakish smile.

We seek connections with the strange and communion with brave souls seeking the truth—not the entire truth, just a piece of it will do—a coin of truth we can keep in a pocket near our valuables, that we can spend in those frightening moments when we don't know ourselves, when we're in too deep and some clarity would help, some beauty that could redeem and enliven the night.

We turn awful experience and bad relationships and murdering office jobs and loveless parents and poverty and addictions and angst and loss and death itself into the fearsome gold of art.

We are alchemists and con artists, acrobats and used-car sales-men, liars and enlighteners, and we are here to do the earth's bidding because the earth is screaming out its stories and begging for us to write them down, and act them out, and draw her pretty pictures on the face of the clouds.

What's in store now that you've made it through this training ground of the imagination?

Here are some of the highs and lows you can expect on this amazing journey.

There's joy as you travel to wonderful places and receive the smiles and affection of new friends made in the crucible of performance, in front of raging armies of critics and prove-it-to-me-I've-paid-too-much-for-these-tickets-I-saw-it-last-year-in-London audiences, and a perfect stranger comes up to you after the show to say they never felt so transported in the theatre before and they understand something about life they never understood until tonight and how you captured her parents' pain and nobility so beautifully.

Fatigue as you give it everything you have, every single day, every muscle engaged in a marathon that doesn't end until you end.

Pain because you tell yourself it's just a gig, just a job, but then you fall in love with it anyway.

Discovery of your limits and appreciation for the breathless power of your mastery.

Bliss when you've written that one good sentence; or you delivered that one perfect moment when the lights are on you and only you; or you discover in the text an idea or an image or a parable so true that it makes your audience weep with recognition; or you put out into the world a rendering of a staircase or a costume or a throne of gold in three brilliant dimensions that just last week existed in none.

Awe when you sit backstage, a moment before your entrance and realize you're about to give the greatest soliloquy in our language.

Gratitude when it dawns on you that you make a living from the honey and perspiration of your mind.

Excitement when you write "Act One, Scene One" on the top of the first page; and you sit along the wall on the afternoon of your third callback for your favorite play; and you stand in the back of the house and that moment you worked on for fourteen hours with that actor who never seemed to get it gets the biggest laugh of the night.

Amazement when your lights reflect in the physics of time and space exactly what's happening in the unlit chambers and labyrinths of the hero's soul.

Even more amazement when your project, which you put together with faith, spit and favors turns a remarkable profit in actual U.S. currency.

Humility when you look around and everyone else seems more successful, or richer, or quicker, or better reviewed, or living on both coasts and are equally familiar with Silver Lake and Williamsburg.

Relief when you figure out that, like all great cyclical events in nature, your long career will rise and fall and you'll be hot, then forgotten, then hot, then forgotten, then hot again.

Anger when the words won't cooperate and the costume's too tight and you made a grave error in casting the world premiere, or passion seems to be ebbing, or you'd rather have a baby, or the grant goes to your rival, or that barbarian in the second row keeps texting his lawyer, or ten people show up to your reading in a theatre with three hundred empty seats, or you can't stand Bushwick anymore, or the MacArthur people overlooked you—*again*—or the sitcom's too tempting, or your favorite actor's not available, or the culture's going south while you're going north.

Or maybe you've forgotten something—you forgot the joy and the magic and the purpose and the need for it all.

But then you remember and come back anyway.

That's the amazing part.

You come back the next day because even when the words don't come and the costume's cutting off the blood to your legs, this activity connects you to your most authentic and naked self—to the child who told sweeping sock puppet sagas, and imitated your dad's big laugh, and drew pictures of avenging super heroes, to the adolescent who fell in love with the smell of opening-night flowers, to the mature artist who became enthralled with the great blank space—that enchanted oval on which battles determine the course of history, and lovers learned the key expressions of the heart, and men and women modeled heroism and humanity, and Estragon lost his way, and colored girls considered suicide, and Proctor wouldn't sign his name, and Arial was free to go, and a wicked Moon under a Lorca sky betrayed the idea of love.

You come back to balance art and family, and sometimes your checkbook, because nothing feels as good as the act of acting.

You endure the indifference of agents and literary managers because nothing sounds as nice as the click of that perfect metaphor falling into place.

You put off children, or you put off real estate, or you put off the thousand intangible compromises of the spirit because nothing frees you from the dark enchantments of gravity like this.

You stay up until three in the morning memorizing those sides for your best friend's new play even though she wrote the part for you and the producers insist you have to audition anyway, because nothing brings you closer to Creation that this.

So why do you do these things?

Why come back when it hurts so much?

What kind of people are we?

How crazy do we have to be to put up with this?

Let's face it, given the speed of today's runaway clocks, given the accumulation of power and money in the hands of the very few and all the injustice that flows from that, given the complexity of social intercourse in an age of instant talk and delayed reflection, you're a member of a different species entirely.

You age differently than the rest of the population.

You try hard not to succumb to the common theories and manias of the crowd.

You speak in tongues when everyone else is speaking in fortune cookies.

You make one-of-a-kind little miracles with your bare and blistered hands for below minimum wage as stock markets soar and die and soar and die.

You write about your existential pain in unsentimental words for sentimental audiences.

Your curiosity is so vast and out of control you don't know boundaries and you annoy your lovers with your constant need to analyze their every nuance, and no answer is ever good enough because each answer leads to ten new questions.

You dream in such vivid colors, you wonder if you can market your sleep as the next cool drug.

Your sensitivity to the pain and joy of others is so acute you might as well have multiple personalities.

You and failure are so intimate with each other you could birth one another's bawling babies.

You are gifted and cursed with a love of words so intense few other pleasures can move you like Lopakhin's declaration that he bought the cherry orchard, or what Li'l Bit had to do to learn to drive, or what devils of self-doubt whispered to a beautiful and wounded soul in a psychosis at 4:48 A.M.

For all this and more you came to this school and sacrificed, and worked your ass off, and delayed some big life decisions, and dreamed exceptional dreams, and fertilized your mind, and kept important promises you made to yourself.

That's the important part: you kept the promises you made to yourself to stay in it and learn.

So now that you've come this far, and we're in this room, together, what's my advice? It's not a lot:

> Love grandly.
> Work forcefully.
> Listen humbly.
> Risk intelligently.
> Risk stupidly.
> Scare yourself.
> Recycle your pain.
> Dwell on greatness.
> Make babies and make art for them.
> Slay your heroes.
> Laugh at yourself.
> Betray no one's trust.

Throw parties.

Make time for silence.

Search and search and search and search.

I could go on, but I don't think you need any more advice from me.

I think you're ready.

You, the fighter and hero of this morning's tale are trained and ready to unpack your Heiner Müller and your tap shoes and your colored pencils, and are brimming with ideas and full of courage and full of fight and you know the obstacles and laugh in their faces, and the dragons you fight are windmills and the windmills you fight are straw and the time to talk about doing it is over.

It's time to do it.

So let's go out now, you and I, let's go out and make some art.

Thank you, and all the best of luck.

José Rivera

Adena Rivera-Dundas

José Rivera is the author of some thirty plays and twenty screenplays translated into scores of languages and seen around the world.

Playwriting honors include two Obie Awards (for *Marisol* and *References to Salvador Dalí Make Me Hot*, both produced by the Public Theater, New York), a Whiting Foundation Award, a McKnight Fellowship, a Rockefeller Foundation Grant and a Kennedy Center Grant. On a Fulbright Arts Fellowship he was writer-in-residence at the Royal Court Theatre in London. He has served as a Creative Advisor for the Sundance Screenwriting Lab in Utah, Jordan and India.

His plays have premiered Off-Broadway and have been seen at virtually every major theatre in the U.S. They include *The House of Ramón Iglesia*, *The Promise*, *Each Day Dies with Sleep*, *Cloud Tectonics*, *Sueño*, *The Street of the Sun*, *Giants Have Us in Their Books*, *Sonnets for an Old Century*, *Brainpeople*, *Adoration of the Old Woman*, *School of the Americas*, *Massacre (Sing to Your Children)*, *Boleros for the Disenchanted*, *Human Emotional Process*, *The Book of Fishes* and *The Hours Are Feminine*.

In 2005 Rivera became the first Puerto Rican nominated for an Academy Award in screenwriting for his first produced screenplay, *The Motorcycle Diaries*, directed by Walter Salles. His film adaptation of Jack Kerouac's *On the Road*, also directed by Salles, will premiere worldwide in 2012.

In the works are a new translation of *The Kiss of the Spider Woman*, a musical set in the Colombian women's prison, Buen Pastor, for the Civilians theatre company and *Love Makes the City Crumble*, his first novel. Rivera lives in New York with his wife, actress and director Sona Tatoyan.